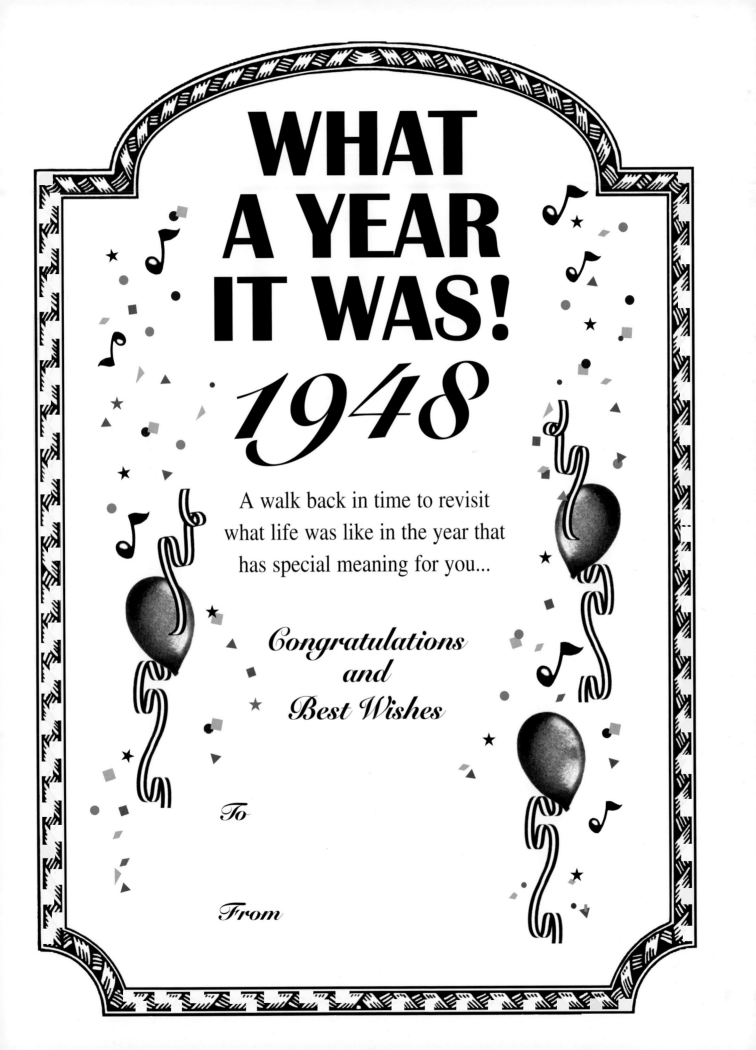

DEDICATION

To My Friend Kenny Bookbinder...
One Of The Great Entrepreneurs Of Our Day.
Happy "Big 5-0" Kenny!

Designer • Peter Hess
Research and Production Supervisor • Laurie Cohn

CONTENTS

TRUMAN ADDRESSES CONGRESS ON STATE OF UNION

The President asks for the immediate passage of the first step of the Marshall Plan and offers his own program for fighting inflation and reducing taxes.

Truman receives standing ovation from Congress.

1948
Politics and World Events

President Truman shakes hands with the Speaker of the House Joe Martin before beginning his talk. On the left is Vice-President Alben W. Barkley.

HIGHLIGHTS OF HIS SPEECH:

"High prices must not be our means of rationing…"

"We must deal effectively and at once with the high cost of living…"

"We must stop the spiral of inflation…"

"A cost of living tax credit should be extended to our people consisting of a credit of $40 to each individual taxpayer with an additional $40 for each dependent…"

"When we have conquered inflation, we shall move forward to our chosen goals. As we do so let us keep ever before us our high purposes…"

President Truman and his entourage arrive at the Capitol for his address to a Joint Session of Congress.

TRUMAN SIGNS THE FOREIGN ASSISTANCE ACT

Under terms of Marshall Plan European organization for economic cooperation is formed.

Flanked by members of his Cabinet and the U.S. Congress, President Truman signs the Foreign Assistance Act which activates the Marshall Plan for European economic recovery.

"...The Foreign Assistance Act is the best answer this country can make in reply to the vicious and distorted misrepresentations of our efforts for peace... This measure is America's answer to the challenge facing the free world today..."

IKE

A Procession For General Eisenhower.

Ike is cheered as his entourage moves through the streets of Philadelphia.

WHAT A YEAR IT WAS!

BACKS MARSHALL PLAN

The General receives a Lifetime Achievement Award from the Poor Richard's Club of Philadelphia.

"...**E**urope never made a better investment than the money and supplies sent at Franklin's behest to help this struggling nation..."

"...**A** tremendous modern complex that has delivered so much to the world and which twice has gone back to Europe to preserve freedom ... that is one of the results of that great investment of that day..."

Ike addresses the assemblage and thanks them for the honor bestowed on him.

"...**P**erhaps if we, in our lifetime, investing in the other direction can achieve some comparable results, that age-old, that century-old hope of all mankind that this peace which we have now gained may be without end may at last be reality..."

"...**A**gain I say, I am exceedingly proud to represent all the men who wore the uniform of the Army in World War II and to be here today and receive this award..."

Harold E. Stassen Sweeps Wisconsin Vote Winning Over N.Y. Governor Thomas E. Dewey And General Douglas MacArthur In Republican Presidential Primary.

Dewey receives no delegates but is still in the race.

General Douglas MacArthur picks up 8 of the delegates.

Voters go to the polls to select 27 delegates to the Republican Convention.

Stassen picks up 19 of the delegates.

WHAT A YEAR IT WAS!

Truman On The Presidential Campaign Trail

President Truman Accepts Democratic Presidential Nomination With Senator Alben W. Barkley Of Kentucky As The Vice-Presidential Candidate.

President Truman, along with Mrs. Truman and his running mate, Alben Barkley, embark on a cross-country campaign of their own.

Touring grass roots country of the midwest Truman attends an Agricultural Festival at Dexter, Iowa featuring a National Plowing Match.

President Truman's Whistle Stop Tour Proves Successful With American Voters As He Travels Over 31,000 Miles Speaking To Over 12 Million People.

Republicans Nominate New York's Governor Thomas E. Dewey As Presidential Candidate And California's Governor Earl Warren As His Running Mate In First Televised Convention.

Dewey On The Presidential Campaign Trail

Albany puts its best foot forward as it welcomes Republican presidential candidate Governor Thomas E. Dewey as he sets forth on his campaign tour with Mrs. Dewey.

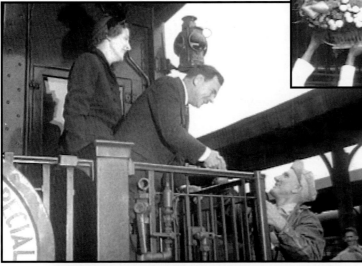

Governor Dewey tries to convince the voters to oust the Democrats after 16 years of Democrat Presidents.

In One Of The Major Upsets In American Political History, President Truman Defies Predictions Of A Republican Landslide And Wins Full Term In White House Defeating Republican Thomas E. Dewey.

BOTH THE DEMOCRATS AND REPUBLICANS TRY TO WOO DWIGHT D. EISENHOWER FOR THE PRESIDENCY.

DEMOCRATS
Ban Race Segregation In National Headquarters In Bid For Negro* Support.

*Negro was the commonly used term in 1948 and is used throughout this book.

Mundt-Nixon Bill
Approved By Congress Requiring Communists To Register With The Government. Henry Wallace Blasts Bill As Cold War Aggression Against The Soviet Union.

Thousands March In Washington To Demand Defeat Of Mundt-Nixon Bill.

Taft-Hartley Ban On Political Spending By Unions Nullified By Federal District Court.

Washington Forces C.I.O. To Eliminate Members Who Oppose Marshall Plan.

$6.2 BILLION FOREIGN AID BILL PASSED BY HOUSE.

Senator Vandenberg Receives Senate Applause As He Calls For Speed-Up Of European Relief To Avert Third World War.

Maryland's Margaret Chase Smith Becomes First Republican Woman To Win A Full Senate Term.

In Grass Lake, Michigan Women Win All Nine Village Council Seats.

STALIN Supports Truman Opponent Henry Wallace.

Southern Democrats Form States' Rights Party (Dixiecrats) In Opposition To Truman's Civil Rights Policies.

Nashville Star Roy Acuff Unsuccessfully Runs For Governor Of Tennessee.

NEW SENATE KIDS ON THE BLOCK
Hubert Humphrey (D-Minnesota)
Lyndon Baines Johnson (D-Texas)

Oliver Hill Becomes Richmond, Virginia's First Negro Councilman.

The California Supreme Court Declares Ban On Interracial Marriages Is Unconstitutional.

U.S. Supreme Court Rules Preventing Minorities From Owning Real Estate Is A Violation Of The 14th Amendment.

An Alabama Jury Gives A 45 Year Sentence To Two White Men For Raping A Negro.

PRESIDENT TRUMAN RECEIVES HERO'S WELCOME IN VIRGIN ISLANDS AS SUPPORTER OF ISLANDER'S RIGHTS.

President Truman Criticizes The Displaced Persons Act Authorizing The Admission Of 205,000 European Refugees Into The United States As Being "Flagrantly Discriminatory" Against Jews And Catholics.

President Truman Assails "Jim Crowism" And Calls On Congress To Outlaw Lynching And To Establish A Federal Commission On Civil Rights.

Truman Proposes Second Largest Peacetime Budget (Over $39.6 Billion) In Nation's History.

To Fight Inflation, Truman Asks For Price-Control Powers.

PRESIDENT TRUMAN PLEDGES TO MAKE A DEADLIER A-BOMB AS SOVIETS PURSUE INTERNATIONAL CONTROL.

UNITED NATIONS

- U.N. Trusteeship Council boycott by Soviets ends after 13 months.

- Soviets veto U.N. proposal to lift Berlin blockade.

- U.N. approves plan for atom control rejecting Soviet proposal.

- U.S. prevents Spain's admittance to U.N.

*T*he United Nations Adopts
THE UNIVERSAL DECLARATION OF HUMAN RIGHTS:

"The declaration, adopted by the General Assembly in 1948, proclaims for men and women everywhere the right to life, liberty and security; freedom from slavery and from arbitrary arrests and detention; and rights including a fair trial."

After Three Years Of Tireless Work,
ELEANOR ROOSEVELT
Receives Standing Ovation As The U.N. General Assembly Adopts The Human Rights Declaration.

General Bradley Becomes New Army Chief

General Omar Bradley is sworn in as new Army Chief of Staff.

President Truman looks on as General Dwight D. Eisenhower congratulates his successor.

President Truman pins a Third Cluster on General Eisenhower's Distinguished Service Medal as he retires after two brilliant years as Chief of Staff and 35 years of Army service during which he commanded the greatest Armed Forces in the world's history.

President Truman congratulates Ike on his commendable service.

MOSCOW charges Sweden of offering military bases to U.S.

SOVIET Union prepares to close its only U.S. Consulates—in New York and San Francisco.

FILIPINO President Manuel Roxas dies of heart attack in Manila.

KONRAD Adenauer leads formation of Parliamentary Council in Bonn.

BERLIN city hall seized by rioting communists.

MILDRED Elizabeth Gillars, known as "Axis Sally," indicted for treason in Washington.

WASHINGTON recognizes South Korea naming John Muccio ambassador.

U.S. abandons plan to decentralize Japanese industry.

CARDINAL Joseph Mindszenty arrested in Budapest for alleged plot against government.

MARTIAL law proclaimed in Indonesia.

FAMOUS BIRTHS

Al Gore
Tipper Gore
Justice Clarence Thomas
Garry Trudeau

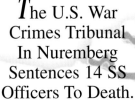
The 23-Nation General Agreement On Trade And Tariffs Designed To Reduce International Trade Barriers Goes Into Effect.

Britain's Prime Minister Attlee Accuses Soviets Of Threatening Europe With New Imperialism.

In A Speech In Wales, Winston Churchill Implores The U.S. To Keep Its Atomic Bomb For World Security From Communism.

Ireland's Fianna Fail Loses Majority After 16 Years In Power – Eamon de Valera Resigns As Prime Minister As John A. Costello Takes Over Leadership.

Rumanian King Michael Breaks Silence Saying His Abdication Was Not Voluntary.

For The First Time Since 1522 Greece Regains Control Over 50 Dodecanese Aegean Islands.

Egypt's King Farouk Lays Cornerstone On New Dam On Upper Nile.

The U.S. Sixth Fleet Begins Operation In Mediterranean Waters.

The U.S. War Crimes Tribunal In Nuremberg Sentences 14 SS Officers To Death.

Despite Violence Set Off By Assassination Of Liberal Leader Jorge Gaitan In Bogota, Colombia, Delegates From 21 Countries Sign Charter Of The Organization Of American States Which Provides For Common Defense And The Peaceful Settlement Of Hemispheric Issues.

Argentina's Juan Peron Accuses U.S. Ex-Diplomat Of Murder Plot Stirring Anti-American Sentiment.

Romulo Gallegos Wins Venezuela's First Presidential Election, Holds Office Until He Is Overthrown By A Military Coup In November.

Soviets Control Western Trains Bound For Berlin.

U.S. Begins Airlifting Supplies To Berlin To Counter Soviet Attempts To Block Ally Efforts.

U.S., Britain And France Pledge To Keep Troops In Germany "Until Peace In Europe Is Secured."

In Washington Bernard Baruch Tells Senate Committee "We Are In The Midst Of A Cold War Which Is Getting Warmer."

Russian Commanders Tighten Blockade Around Allied Sectors Of Berlin But Allies Are Determined To Provide Supplies To Prevent Starvation. Nearly 3/4 Of A Million Tons Of Food Flown In.

Communist Chief Palmiro Togliatti Assassinated In Rome—Riots Sweep Italy.

EVENTS 1948

YUGOSLAVIA Marshall Tito Accuses Russia Of Trying To Topple His Government And Breaks With Moscow. Tito Announces His Country Will Follow His Own Communist Line.

PRAGUE

In A Coup D'Etat Czech Communists Topple Government And Seize Control.

President Edward Benes Capitulates To Communist Leader, Prime Minister Clement Gottwald.

U.S., France And Britain Condemn Prague Coup.

Prague Bans Foreign Press And 27 Publications.

Foreign Minister Jan Masaryk's Suicide Thought By Many To Be Murder.

*H*ikedi Tojo, The Leader Responsible For Plunging Japan Into World War II, Is Sentenced By An International Tribunal To Hang For War Crimes Along With Six Collaborators.

*N*orth Korea Adopts Constitution Claiming Sovereignty For All Korea.

*S*oviet Tanks Move Into Berlin.

*S*hanghai-Born Jews Arrive In Israel.

*I*n Seoul, South Korea Syngman Rhee Claims Sovereignty For All Korea.

*D*utch Troops, Disregarding A United Nations Cease-Fire Order, Capture Last Indonesian Republic Stronghold. Achmed Sukarno Arrested.

*P*remier Alcide de Gasperi's Christian Democratic Party Wins 48% Of The Vote In Italy's First Election Under Its New Constitution.

*S*enator Luigi Einaudi Becomes Italy's First President.

CHINA

Neither Chiang Kai-shek's New Presidency Nor New Constitution Is Thwarting The Communists In Their Territorial Expansion.

Madame Chiang Kai-shek Arrives In Washington Seeking U.S. Aid.

*T*he Right-Wing Nationalist Party, Which Includes Neo-Nazis, Has Ousted Jan Christiaan Smuts, Prime Minister Of South Africa, From Office. This Is The Beginning Of The Apartheid Policy.

*O*ver 661,000 World War II Prisoners Of War Are Released.

*P*oland's People's Workers Party Chief Ousted For Advocating Independence From Moscow.

*F*rench Bring First Nuclear Reactor Into Service.

Formation Of North China People's Government Announced On Communist Radio In Nanking.

Nationalist China Concedes Manchuria Lost To Reds.

WHAT A YEAR IT WAS!

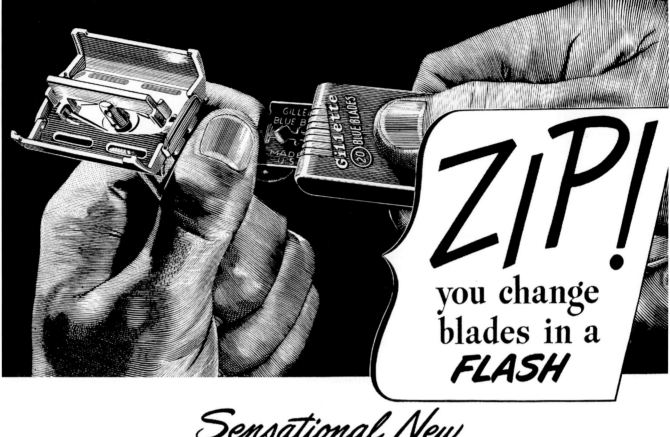

ZIP!
you change blades in a *FLASH*

Sensational New
Gillette Dispenser

Puts 20 Gillette Blue Blades With 40 Super-Keen Shaving Edges at Your Finger Tips!

YOU deal out a new Gillette Blue Blade *instantly* with the amazing new Gillette Dispenser... shave quicker than ever. The handy plastic case holds blades firmly... keeps their edges *factory-sharp*. When the Dispenser is empty... discard it. You pay nothing extra for the Gillette Dispenser ... only the usual price for 20 blades. Gillette Safety Razor Company. *(Prices apply in U.S.A. only.)*

For use with any Gillette Razor
20 Gillette BLUE BLADES
King C. Gillette
MADE IN U.S.A.

20 Blades 40 Shaving Edges 98¢

Special Introductory Offer

Gillette Super-Speed One-Piece Razor and Gillette Dispenser with 10 Gillette Blue Blades

REGULAR $1⁵⁰ VALUE

$1⁰⁰

The Greatest Shaving Bargain On Earth!

See Your Nearest Retailer

● You enjoy utmost shaving comfort and convenience with this brand new Gillette Super-Speed Razor Set. Twist... the razor opens. Zip ...there's a new blade. Twist again... and start shaving. Cleaning's no problem either... just loosen holder, rinse and shake the moisture out.

look *SHARP!* feel *SHARP!* be *SHARP!* use Gillette Blue Blades
WITH THE *SHARPEST* EDGES EVER HONED

WASHINGTON FEELS THE REPERCUSSIONS OF THE RED COUP IN CZECHOSLOVAKIA.

Ambassador Uri Slovak winds up his affairs after resigning and vows to lead the fight for the reinstatement of a democratic regime in his homeland.

At the Czech Embassy in Washington a political crisis is reached as the staff prepares to leave in protest against the Communist takeover.

From his farm in Virginia Premiere Imre Nagy makes the following statement:

"As Premiere of Hungary, I saw the free people of my country subjected to the Communist domination the same way that it has now effected the people of Czechoslovakia. The nations remaining free now must watch for the beginnings of the same Communist danger in their own lands."

U.N. MEDIATOR SLAIN BY ASSASSIN'S BULLETS

Count Folke Bernadotte, man of peace and mediator for the United Nations, is the victim of a hail of bullets in ancient Jerusalem.

"Lend me your ears" *says science*

It's no accident that you hear so clearly when you pick up your telephone. Bell Laboratories engineers are constantly at work to make listening easy for you.

When these engineers design a method to bring speech still more clearly to your ears, the new circuit is given many scientific tests. Then it gets a final check from a "Sounding Board" like the one pictured above.

This check shows just how the system will work in actual use. The men and women represent you and many millions of other telephone listeners. Their trained ears check syllables, words and sentences as they come over the telephones. While they listen, they write down their ratings.

The Board members give approval only when they are sure that the voice they hear is natural in tone, clear in quality and easily understood. Not until they are certain the circuit will suit your ear is it put into use.

BELL TELEPHONE SYSTEM

 BELL TELEPHONE LABORATORIES *A great research organization, working to bring you the best possible telephone service at the lowest possible cost*

18

MAHATMA GANDHI ASSASSINATED BY HINDU EXTREMIST

Mohandas K. Gandhi, 78-year old spiritual leader of Indian independence for more than 20 years, is shot and killed by a fanatical Hindu opposed to Gandhi's message of peace and non-violence. Over 1 million people observe the scattering of Gandhi's ashes in the Ganges river at Allahabad.

In a radio speech to the nation, Prime Minister Pandit Jawaharlal Nehru's quivering voice said: *"Gandhi has gone out of our lives and there is darkness everywhere..."* The news of his death set off riots in Bombay and other cities. The assassination follows Gandhi's recent 121-hour fast to halt Moslem-Hindu riots.

Burma
Gains Independence After 62 Years Of British Rule.

Last British Troops Leave India.

Ceylon Becomes Independent.

Pakistan Accuses India Of Campaign To Annihilate Moslems. Both Nations Accept U.N. Mediation.

Commanding General Rana, Nepal's Envoy To U.S., Received By President Truman.

1948

PALESTINE UNREST

In a tense atmosphere, the Security Council of the United Nations meets in Lake Success, Long Island to debate the resolution put forth by American Delegate Warren Austin to have the council endorse the Palestine Partition Edict.

In a last minute effort to find a solution by conciliation between the Arabs and Jews, Canada's Delegate General McNaughton addresses the Assembly.

An overwrought American spectator demonstrating against any use of force involving American troops to compel partition is forcibly removed from the council chamber.

NEW JEWISH STATE FORMED AMID STRIFE

TEL AVIV – MAY 14th: State Of Israel Proclaimed. Prime Minister David Ben Gurion Reads Proclamation As Israeli Flag Flies Overhead.

Israelis joyously waving at their new flag.

1948

HOSTILITIES IN PALESTINE

Cleanup after bomb explodes on Ben Yehuda Street in Jerusalem.

A young blast victim cries for his mother.

Volunteers looking for survivors buried in the rubble.

First aid is given to the injured.

A human chain prevents people from entering the bombed area during cleanup.

Soldiers put out a fire.

Israeli soldiers and armed civilians patrol the streets.

Israelis searching for Palestinian terrorists.

Israeli woman displaced by terrorist acts.

United States Delegate Warren Austin.

EMERGENCY MEETING OF THE U.N. PALESTINE COMMISSION

Spectators watch the proceedings at the United Nations.

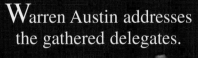

Warren Austin addresses the gathered delegates.

"If the Security Council should decide that it is necessary to use armed force to maintain international peace in connection with Palestine, the United States will be ready to consult under the charter with a view to such action as may be necessary to maintain international peace. But this action must be directed solely to the maintenance of international peace. The Council's action in other words is directed to keeping the peace and not to enforcing partition."

JANUARY

JERUSALEM: Bomb Blast At Arab Higher Committee Office Kills 14 And Injures 98.

FEBRUARY

HAIFA: Jews And Arabs Escalate Fighting As Immigration Of Jewish Refugees Increases. Zionist Fighters Claim Death Of 82 Arabs.

JERUSALEM: 33 Killed In Jewish Quarter As Heavy Explosion Destroys Ben Yehuda Street.

PALESTINE: Stern Gang, Jewish Terrorist Unit, Blows Up Cairo-Haifa Train, Killing 30 British Soldiers.

MARCH

JERUSALEM: Right To Mobilize U.S. Citizens Claimed By Zionist Militia Haganah.

JERUSALEM: Powerful Explosion Rocks Headquarters Of The Jewish Agency For Palestine Killing 11 And Wounding 86.

APRIL

HAIFA: Arabs Surrender To The Haganah And Evacuate Haifa After Fierce Fighting.

LAKE SUCCESS: Jewish Representative Tells U.N. That Following End Of British Mandate On May 16th A Jewish State In Palestine Will Become A Reality Regardless Of Any U.N. Action On Partition.

NEW YORK: Arabs Threaten Independent State If U.N. Fails To Establish Trusteeship Over Palestine.

MAY

NEW YORK: Syrian Army Invades Palestine – Jewish Agency Demands U.N. Action.

TEL AVIV – MAY 14th: State Of Israel Proclaimed. Prime Minister David Ben Gurion Reads Proclamation As Israeli Flag Flies Overhead. Dr. Chaim Weizmann Elected Provisional President. Israel Opens Its Door To All Jews.

TEL AVIV: Egypt Bombs Tel Aviv As It Invades Israel.

TEL AVIV: Troops From Five Arab Nations Invade Israel.

NEW YORK: American Zionist Emergency Council Holds "Salute To Israel" Rally In Madison Square Garden – Tens Of Thousands Are Turned Away.

NEW YORK: U.N. Names Count Folke Bernadotte Mediator For Palestine.

PALESTINE: Four Egyptian Spitfires Downed By The British.

CONFLICT...CONFLICT.

MIDDLE...EAST...1948

JUNE

TRANSJORDAN: Israeli Planes Blast Amman.

ISRAEL: Arabs And Jews Sign Armistice.

TRIPOLI: State Of Emergency Declared To Quell Riots Between Arabs And Jews.

NEW YORK: U.N. Rejects Soviet Request To Send Official Observers To Palestine.

JULY

ISRAEL: Egypt Attacks Israel By Air, Iraq By Land Breaking Arab Month-Long Truce.

CAIRO: Bowing To U.N. Pressure, Israelis And Arabs Agree To Truce In Jerusalem.

AUGUST

PALESTINE: Israeli Army Halts Egyptian Drive Across "No Man's Land."

SEPTEMBER

JERUSALEM: U.N. Mediator For Palestine, Count Folke Bernadotte And U.N. Aide Assassinated By Jewish Irregulars As Their Car Drives Through Israeli-Occupied Area Of Jerusalem.

OCTOBER

ISRAEL: Arab-Israeli Fighting Resumes Ending Truce.

ISRAEL: Israelis Capture Beersheba.

VATICAN: Pope Pius XII Urges International Jerusalem.

NEW YORK: President Truman Takes Powerful Pro-Israel Stand In Madison Square Garden Speech Vowing That Israel Must "Be Large Enough, Free Enough And Strong Enough To Make Its People Self-Supporting And Secure."

NOVEMBER

ISRAEL: Egyptians Retreat From Negev On U.N. Order – Israelis Defy.

DECEMBER

BEIRUT: Arab Leaders Name Abdullah Hussein Of Transjordan King Of Palestine.

NEW YORK: Israel's Bid For U.N. Membership Is Rejected By The Security Council Because Of Abstentions By France And Canada.

ISRAEL: Blackout Throughout Country Following Arab Air Raids.

...CONFLICT...

Why is going Pullman like...

...a visit with friends?

1. Because you're *always* a welcome guest when you go Pullman. No matter what your accommodations, the friendly Pullman conductor and porter are at your service.

...a night out?

2. Because you can meet new people, make new friends, see new places — as you relax and enjoy yourself in the luxurious lounge car reserved for Pullman passengers.

...a night at home?

3. Because you have almost all of the comforts of home when you go Pullman. A big, soft, comfortable bed. Clean, modern toilet facilities. And — on longer trips — delicious meals are available.

...a lock on your door?

4. Because going Pullman — like the lock on your door — gives you that *safe* feeling. Fact is, you're safer crossing the country by Pullman than you are crossing the street in your home town.

...a happy ending?

5. Because your Pullman trip ends happily. You arrive as fresh as you left ... on dependable railroad schedules ... right in the heart of town ... convenient to everything.

Go Pullman

THE **SAFEST**, MOST **COMFORTABLE** WAY
TO **GET THERE!**

The National Guard Defends America — Join Now!

© 1948, THE PULLMAN COMPANY

VOYAGE TO 1948 FREEDOM

EUROPEAN JEWS ON THEIR VOYAGE TO PALESTINE.

FACES OF THE REFUGEES REFLECT HOPE AND EXCITEMENT ABOUT REACHING THE PROMISED LAND.

A refugee takes a break from reading.

Living conditions in hold of ship.

Making the best of limited sanitary facilities.

WHAT A YEAR IT WAS!

27

VOYAGE TO
A BRITISH GUNBOAT

Jews are hidden under tarps as British patrol planes pass overhead.

The long and strenuous voyage takes its toll on some passengers.

The coast is clear for the moment.

FREEDOM CONTINUED 1948
PATROLS THE WATERS

The phony name of the ship gets tossed into the sea.

British soldiers board the refugee tanker.

Despite all the adversities, the refugees are determined to begin their new lives in Palestine.

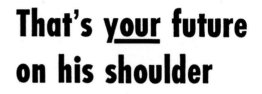

That's <u>your</u> future on his shoulder

That small gold bar spells security for you. Security and peace of mind and the kind of life you want for yourself and for your family.

It means something more, too. It means that America is and will always be the land of opportunity. For this young officer was just an average American boy when he enlisted. With the average ambition to get ahead, to have financial security, to hold a job. And now he's an executive in the nation's most important business.

The way up to the rank of second lieutenant wasn't a breeze. A man in this big job must know how to bring out the best in every blessed man under him . . . how to keep his head while he listens with his heart to some young fellow's personal problems . . . how to train and teach others, yet never stop learning himself.

To men who want to be the leaders of tomorrow the U. S. Army offers the opportunities of a lifetime. The greatest chance for advancement. And a career that commands respect the world over.

PEACE IS AMERICA'S MOST IMPORTANT BUSINESS

The new peacetime Army and Air Force offer Young Men . . .

★ WIDEST CHOICE OF CAREER JOBS
★ BEST OPPORTUNITY FOR ADVANCEMENT
★ UNUSUAL RETIREMENT BENEFITS

U.S. ARMY and **U.S. AIR FORCE**
RECRUITING SERVICE

PEOPLE

IKE & MAMIE
BECOME GRANDPARENTS

Ike and Mamie Beam As They Visit Their First Grandchild, David Dwight II, Born At West Point's Military Hospital.

IKE & MAMIE

Mamie straightens Ike's tie.

Ike signs autographs for military personnel.

Mamie smiles lovingly at Ike.

Photographers Take Advantage Of The Opportunity To Snap The Eisenhowers As They Leave Their Home.

1948 PRESIDENT TRUMAN PAYS VISIT TO CARIBBEAN

Enthusiastic Citizens Line The Street To Get A Glimpse Of President Truman.

The President holds up plaque he is awarded as a Champion of Human Rights.

MARGARET TRUMAN LAUNCHES THE HARRY TRUMAN IN TWO PARTS

Margaret Truman takes time out of her singing career as she arrives in New Orleans to launch a river tugboat bearing her father's name.

A crowd assembles on the dock to watch the festivities.

The christening turns out to be in two parts with Margaret launching the tugboat first with the traditional bottle of champagne.

Margaret then christens the Harry S. Truman and sends the boat on its watery way.

THE FLYING TIGER TAKES A WIFE

Chinese newspaper-woman, 24-year old Anna Chan, becomes bride of Flying Tiger Major General Claire Chennault.

A staunch defender of China during her darkest hours, the romance, which brings the General his second wife, culminated against a backdrop of China fighting for her life. The General is now head of China's Air Relief Service.

Anna's sister, Cynthia, one-time nurse to the Flying Tigers, gives her a warm hug.

In California, Air Force Major Richard Johnson (Right) Gets Ready To Fly A Production Model Of An F-86 Jet Fighter (Below) And Breaks The World's Speed Record By Reaching 671 M.P.H.

WHAT A YEAR IT WAS!

NATIONAL BOND DRIVE KICKS OFF IN NEW YORK

Sparking the national drive for the Treasury Security Loan campaign, a gala opening of "ARE YOU WITH IT?" draws thousands to a bond rally in New York.

Thousands pay the price of admission for National Security which is the purchase of either a $25, $100 or $1,000 Government Bond.

Donald O'Connor, star of "ARE YOU WITH IT?" hands over the day's receipts to Louis Pierson, New York Chairman of the Bond Drive, as president of Universal International John J. O'Connor looks on.

King George and Queen Elizabeth welcome Eleanor Roosevelt to London on her arrival to unveil a statue of her late husband, Franklin.

GEORGE MARSHALL

Secretary George Marshall receives Humanitarian Award from the Variety Clubs of America for his great contribution to world peace.

The Secretary and his wife get ready to leave for France to deal with a long list of world problems.

WHAT A YEAR IT WAS!

The Queen Elizabeth

Steams Into New York Harbor Carrying European Celebrities.

Ex-King Michael of Rumania and his mother are the center of attraction.

Facing a press battery King Michael says that the Reds forced his resignation and that nothing short of war will restore his regime and voices his keen anticipation about his first visit to the United States.

Famous British director, J. Arthur Rank, arrives with his wife for his second visit in the past year. During his stay, Mr. Rank plans to attend to business connected to his extensive motion picture interests in the U.S. and hopes to visit Hollywood.

Olympic champions Dick Button and Gretchen Fraser arrive after a triumphant performance at the Winter Olympics.

1948

HOLLYWOOD SCULPTOR YUCCA SALAMUNICH PICKS LEGS HE ADMIRES

Hedy Lamarr
Alexis Smith
Ray Bolger
Jane Russell
Citation
A Chippendale Chair

A LEG UP

According to Marlene Dietrich the average man is more interested in a woman who is interested in him than he is in a woman with beautiful legs – although beautiful legs help.

Jimmy Durante

Receives A Heart Of Gold Award From The Men's Club Of Mount Sinai National Medical Center In California.

There's MONEY In Them There WORDS

Dr. William Carlos Williams Receives $1,000 Award From The National Institute Of Arts And Letters.

British Amateur Golf Champion Frank Stranahan Is Awakened By A Burglar, Grabs A No. 3 Iron And Convinces The Intruder Not To Move Until The Police Come.

FAMOUS BIRTH
Richard Simmons

MARLENE DIETRICH'S 10 MOST FASCINATING MEN

Erich Maria Remarque
Alexander Kirk
Igor Stravinsky
Ernest Hemingway
Roberto Rossellini
Pablo Picasso
Erle Stanley Gardner
Salvador Dali
Noel Coward
Arturo Toscanini

The Mouse Turns 21

Walt Disney Celebrates Mickey Mouse's 21st Birthday With A Quiet Dinner Honoring The Best-Known Star In The World— Veteran Of More Pictures Than Any Actor In Hollywood.

1948

THE CHIPS ARE DOWN

Testifying At An Income Tax Evasion Trial Of A Chicago Gambler, Bud Abbott & Lou Costello Are Asked How Much They Lost At Poker.

Bud: $20,000-$25,000.
Lou: $15,000

THE ULTIMATE ACTING JOB

Bob Hope Named Honorary Mayor Of Palm Springs, California While Bing Crosby Is Chosen Mayor Of Elko, Nevada.

Esther Williams Denounces The Tiny Bathing Suit Declaring That They Come Off In The Water Making Them Unsuitable For Swimming.

MAKING A BIG SPLASH

THAR SHE BLOWS

Mr. & Mrs. Gregory Peck, Boating In Their Cruiser "Tonga," Are Rescued By The Coast Guard In Turbulent Waters Off The Miami Coast.

THIS HAS A FAMILIAR RING TO IT

Young Starlet Lila Leeds Is Being Sued By Her Ex-Fiance For Return Of His $1,000 Engagement Ring.

The Lady Is Kissed Off

Actress Jacqua Lynn Wins An Annulment Of Her Marriage To Paul Haertel On The Grounds That Not Only Did He Not Kiss Her On Their Wedding Night, But Has Not Kissed Her In Their 28 Months Of Marriage.

BREAKING BREAD INSTEAD OF EACH OTHER'S HEAD

Feuding Hollywood Gossip Columnists Hedda Hopper And Louella Parsons Shock Lunchtime Diners When They Are Seen Together At Romanoff's In Hollywood. The Reason For Burying The Hatchet (And Not In Each Other) Is Hedda's Favorable Review Of Louella's Daughter's Picture "I Remember Mama."

A GENTLEMEN'S BURGLAR

The Tenth Duke & Duchess Of Rutland Packed A Little Lighter For Their Planned Trip To South Africa After A Burglar Broke Into Their London House And Stole $28,000 In Furs And Jewelry. The Burglars Took A Bit Of Time Before Leaving To Enjoy A Few Apples And The Duke's Best Scotch.

WHAT A YEAR IT WAS!

ROME
Celebrates Pope Pius XII's 72nd Birthday.

Despite The Level Of Sophistication Of Today's Young Woman, Pope Pius Warns That She Is No More Protected From "Roguery And Hypocrisy Of Seducers" Than Her Counterparts From The Past.

A KINGDOM, A KINGDOM, A KINGDOM FOR MY KINGDOM

For Defrauding The Rumanian People, Ex-King Michael Is Stripped Of The Following Possessions:

159 Castles   400,000 Acres Of Land
3,991,502 Shares Of Stock
A Couple Of Yachts   Voting Rights

Mother Teresa
Establishes The Missionaries Of Charity Order.

MARTIN LUTHER KING, JR. GRADUATES FROM MOREHOUSE COLLEGE AND IS ORDAINED AT EBENEZER BAPTIST CHURCH IN ATLANTA.

1,000,000 Londoners

Hail King George VI And Queen Elizabeth As They Celebrate Their Silver Wedding Anniversary.

PHILOSOPHER
Bertrand Russell, 76, Survives Norwegian Flying Boat Crash By Swimming In The Icy Sea Off The Norwegian Coast.

I SEE A BIG CHANGE IN THE FUTURE

Joseph Stalin Donates A Crystal Ball Made From Glassworkers At The Sklara Poremba Factory.

A ROYAL ITCH

The Royal Physician Isolates Princess Margaret From Her Sister Elizabeth During Margaret's Bout With The Measles.

Great-Great-Grandson Of The One And Only, John Jacob Astor III Is Recuperating From The Measles. Oh Well, He Could Fly To Great Britain And Hang Out With Margaret!

 Happy Birthday Lizzie
Princess Elizabeth Celebrates Her 22nd Birthday With A Family Luncheon And Dinner.

For just about a hundred years,
In this great vale of joy and tears,
The finest foods in all the land
Have borne the name of "Monarch Brand."

More than five hundred finer things
That come in bottle, box and tin,
Are well known for the Lion label
And should be daily on your table.

Here Luke the Lion and Lucy small
Are gazing at the mammoth wall
Of foods so pure, so good, so grand—
This vast array is Monarch Land!

On merchants' shelves (from coast to coast)
Where *best* of quality counts the most
You'll find a stock of Monarch food
To please your every eating mood.

Each day for your own eating pleasure
You should partake of this great treasure.
You'll find the price is strictly right
And *quality* in every bite.

MONA

World's Largest Family of Nationall

RCH

istributed Finer Foods

HONORS

Arriving In New York For His Personal Health After A 5-Year Stint In Hollywood, Playwright Clifford Odets Said It Is Hollywood's Desire "to make every movie as accessible as chewing gum for which no more human maturity of audience is needed than a primitive pair of jaws and a bovine philosophy."

Bernard Baruch Receives 15th Annual Abraham Lincoln Award For Outstanding Public Service From Brooklyn's Abraham Lincoln High School.

Albert Einstein Is Honored With The Wendell Willkie One World Award For His World Citizenship And Hatred Of Militarism, Dictatorship And Violence.

Nelson Rockefeller Receives Citation From National Conference Of Christians And Jews For Good Work In The Field Of Human Relations.

Ernest Hemingway Is Voted One Of "The Most Provocative Faces In The World" By The Artists League Of America. Emperor Hirohito And Ava Gardner's Faces Receive Honorable Mention.

And Yet Another Award To Bernard Baruch – This Time From The American Schools And Colleges Association's Horatio Alger Award For A Fine Ascent From A Lowly Beginning.

After Fathering Six Children, California Governor Earl Warren, 57, Is Named One Of The "Most Virile Men In America" By The International Artists Committee Who Also Name Clark Gable And Victor Mature.

One Of 630 People On King George VI's Honor List, American Poet And Critic **T. S. Eliot** Becomes Only The 25th Person Of High Distinction To Receive The "Order Of Merit," One Of The Crown's Rarest Decorations.

DWIGHT D. EISENHOWER

Though Absent From The Gathering, Dwight D. Eisenhower Is Made Honorary Member Of The Ottawa Indian Tribe In Michigan.

General Dwight D. Eisenhower Takes Over As 13th President Of New York's Columbia University.

THE "BABE" BY ANY OTHER NAME...

Japan Celebrates Its Annual "Babu Rusu Day."

Babe Ruth Presents Yale University Library Manuscript Collection The Manuscript Of His Autobiography "The Babe Ruth Story."

"Babe"

Governors From All 48 States Send Connie Mack, 85, Letters Of Congratulations On His 48th Year As Manager Of The Philadelphia Athletics.

Leo Durocher And His Wife, Loraine Day, Adopt A Little Girl.

HIS HAT'S OFF TO YOU... *Millinery Designers John Harburger And Frederic Hirst Name Joan Crawford Sexiest Hat Wearer While Maria Montez Is Named The Maddest.*

Charlie Chaplin Ordered By Los Angeles Court To Increase Child Support For His Daughter From $75 To $100 Weekly.

We DON'T KAre WHAt YOU SAY AbOUT US, JUST SPELL OUr NaMES XRIGHT

800 Of Hollywood's Most Famous Show Up For Testimonial Dinner Honoring Gossip Columnist Louella Parsons. Among The Notable Absences Are Clark Gable, Cary Grant And Rival Hedda Hopper.

Oveta Culp Hobby Becomes First Woman President Of The Southern Newspaper Publishers Association.

JUST A LITTLE OFF AROUND THE EDGES

Snipped Off Just Before Her Head, Marie Antoinette's Blond Lock Is Auctioned Off In Paris Along With A Brown Cutting From Napoleon, Collected Shortly After His Death On St. Helena.

IS THIS ENOUGH TO MAKE YOUR HAIR CURL?

An upset Jackie Coogan reports the theft of his toupee which he left in the glove compartment of his car.

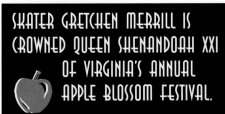

SKATER GRETCHEN MERRILL IS CROWNED QUEEN SHENANDOAH XXI OF VIRGINIA'S ANNUAL APPLE BLOSSOM FESTIVAL.

1948

KIDS NAME THE MOST FAMILIAR FACES IN AMERICA
Dick Tracy / Bing Crosby / Harry Truman

"DIAMOND LIL" LOSES HER DIAMONDS

While Performing In Her Hit Show "Diamond Lil" In London's Prince Of Wales Theatre, Mae West's Dressing Room Is Burglarized And $16,000 Worth Of Diamond Jewelry See Their Last Curtain Call.

HE GOT A KICK OUT OF YOU

Errol Flynn Pays $50 Fine And Apologizes For Kicking A Policeman In The Shins.

MOST POPULAR Cover Girls

Ingrid Bergman

Rita Hayworth

June Allyson

June Haver

Lana Turner

Betty Grable

Shirley Temple

Esther Williams

BING CROSBY
Named Nation's No. 1 Box Office Draw For Fifth Straight Year Followed By

BETTY GRABLE
And

ABBOTT & COSTELLO.

FORMER PRIME MINISTER OF EIRE ARRIVES FOR FIRST VISIT TO NEW YORK IN 28 YEARS.

WITH A SONG IN HER HEART

Jane Froman, Still Recovering From The Airplane Crash Injuries She Sustained In Lisbon, Arrives In Miami To Marry The Co-Pilot John Curtis Burn, Who Despite His Broken Back, Saved Her Life By Keeping Her From Drowning In The Tagus River.

RITA HAYWORTH

Named "Dish Of The Year" By Waiters At The Concord Hotel In Kiamesha Lake, New York.

Fred Astaire & Ginger Rogers

Reunite On The Screen After Ten Years In "The Barkleys Of Broadway."

44

WHAT A YEAR IT WAS!

CECIL B. DeMILLE

Hires Hedy Lamarr
And Victor Mature
To Star In

"SAMSON AND DELILAH."

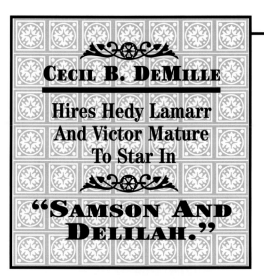

YOU ONE-EYE SON OF A RATTLESNAKE

WHILE HIS BEAUTIFUL WIFE LAUREN BACALL IS FAST ASLEEP, MOVIE TOUGH GUY HUMPHREY BOGART KILLS A RATTLESNAKE OUTSIDE HIS BEVERLY HILLS HOME AFTER IT ATTACKS ONE OF HIS DOGS.

LET THEM EAT CAKE

Addressing An American Legion Luncheon In Tucson, Arizona, Lady Astor Stuns Her Audience By Stating That She Is "Weary of so much talk about the common man and people who are underprivileged."

Lady Astor Loses 14 Pairs Of Her Best Nylons When Burglars Break Into Her Country Home.

¿ YES, BUT CAN SHE ACT ?

Virginia Mayo Selected "Miss Cheesecake Of 1948" By The Stars & Stripes.

YOU GOTTA ROLL WITH THE PUNCHES

Charging that her estranged husband gave her two black eyes as he dragged her out of a bar, a Brooklyn magistrate rules that if women want the privilege of visiting a bar and acting like men, then they have to take a few punches as well.

WHAT'S WRONG WITH THIS OLD RAG?

Deanna Durbin, Barbara Stanwyck And Dorothy Lamour Among Hollywood Designer Ray Driscoll's Ten Worst Dressed Women.

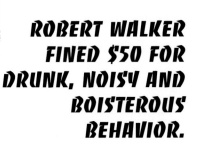

ROBERT WALKER FINED $50 FOR DRUNK, NOISY AND BOISTEROUS BEHAVIOR.

WHAT A YEAR IT WAS!

45

1948 Coupling

Lana Turner & Henry J. "Bob" Topping

Gloria Grahame & Nicholas Ray

Tommy Dorsey & Jane New

William L. Van Duren &
   Kate "Klondike Kate" Rockwell Matson

Edward Dmytryk & Jean Porter

Deposed King Michael of Rumania
   & Princess Anne of Bourbon-Parma

Jose Ferrer & Phyllis Hill

William Randolph Hearst Jr.
   & Austine "Bootsie" McDonnell Cassini

Martha Graham & Erick Hawkins

Ida Lupino & Collier Young

James A. Michener & Vange A. Nord

Winthrop Rockefeller & Barbara Paul Sears,
   "Bobo", a coal miner's daughter

Victor Mature & Dorothy
   Stanford Berry

Issac Stern & Nora Kaye

"Sabu" & Marilyn Cooper

Louis B. Mayer &
   Mrs. Lorena Layson Danker

David Niven & Mrs. Hjordis Tersmeden

Gypsy Rose Lee & Julio de Diego

Uncoupling

William Randolph
   Hearst Jr. &
   Lorelle McCarver
   Swisher Moore Hearst

Mickey Rooney
   & Betty Jane Rase Rooney

Vincent Price
   & Edith Barrett Williams Price

Jane Wyman &
   Ronald Reagan

John Steinbeck &
   Gwyn Conger Steinbeck

Egypt's King Farouk I &
   Queen Farida

Shah of Persia & Empress Fawzia

Margaret Sullavan & Leland Howard

Doris Duke & Porfirio Rubirosa

Artie Shaw & Kathleen Winsor

Ann Sothern & Robert Sterling

Henry B. Du Pont & Margaret Lewis Du Pont

John D. Spreckels III
   & Lou Dell Breese Spreckels

David O. Selznik & Irene Mayer Selznik

Tyrone Power & Annabella

ANNULMENT

*Mrs. Carrie La Rue Rose,
Tiffany heiress
& Don C. Rose*

WHAT A YEAR IT WAS!

SLOW DOWN YOU MOVE TOO FAST

ELLIOTT ROOSEVELT RECEIVES A $10 FINE FOR HIS SECOND SPEEDING TICKET THIS YEAR.

Caryl Chessman Arrested As Possible Suspect In The Red Light Bandit Attacks In New York.

100,000 To 1 Shot

Bernard Baruch Rewards A Race Track Employee For Returning The $2,200 In $100 Bills He Dropped On The Floor.

Much To The Joy Of Many Dubliners, A Statue Of Queen Victoria Is Removed To A Kilmainham Storehouse After 41 Years Of Arousing Their Ire.

DID YOU SAY DROOPY EYES OR "DOPEY" EYES?

Robert Mitchum, whose latest movie "Rachel and the Stranger" is nation's No. 1 box office hit, to stand trial on possession of marijuana.

MRS. GRACE COOLIDGE,

69-Year Old Widow Of The Former President, Comes Out Of Retirement To Attend A World Series Game In Boston.

14-Year Old Harvard Freshman Alexander M. McColl Reveals That He Had Read A 20-Volume Encyclopedia At The Age Of 8.

Women are eligible for degrees from Cambridge University.

Grandma Moses Celebrates Her 88th Birthday With Norman Rockwell Helping Her Cut The Cake Decorated Like One Of Her Paintings.

Poet W. H. Auden is admitted to the most prestigious National Institute of Arts and Letters.

Albert Einstein, 69, Checks Into Brooklyn Hospital For Abdominal Surgery.

PASSINGS:

GENERAL JOHN J. PERSHING, World War I Commander Of The American Expeditionary Forces, Dies At Age 87.

ZELDA FITZGERALD, Widow Of F. Scott Fitzgerald, Dies In A Hospital Fire In Asheville, North Carolina.

WHAT A YEAR IT WAS!

1948

47

COSTUME BY BEN REIG

Cling-cling-cling round your ankles!

CANNON NYLONS give you *extra* elasticity for that smart, hug-the-ankle fit. (And ankles are important these "new look" days.)

Cannons give you misty beauty, too, without a trace of shine (thanks to *high-twist* thread). And because they're made in air-conditioned rooms, every pair's the *same*—in enduring loveliness!

Ask to see BLUHAZE, enchanting new Cannon shade for spring.

not just nylons...but
Cannon Nylons!

CANNON MILLS, INC. ★ Makers of Cannon Towels, Sheets, Blan

Copr. 1948, Cannon Mills.

WALL CUP-VASE
These decorative cup and saucer wall plaques of native American pottery hold plants or flowers without leaking. They're 4½" in diam., and they're available in pink, turquoise, yellow, and wine. You can use these anywhere in your home, and they make a fine gift. Postpaid, pair **1.29**

TRUE OR FALSE
True or false—can you tell? Well, they're artificial, and there's no mess, no dying on the vine with these lifelike ivy and philodendron cuttings. Easily cleaned with a damp cloth. Shape them any way you wish. Generous size. Midget ivy, 25¢ each; regular ivy and philodendron, 69¢ each. Postpaid.

T-BALL TEAPOT
This is a brand-new item, a neatly-designed teapot with side pockets for holding teabags—such a simple idea it's a wonder nobody ever thought of it before. Practical size in attractive assorted colors on native American pottery. Useful and ornamental. postpaid each .. **1.50**

Beautiful new, 36-page, illustrated catalog now available; send 10c in coin to cover handling

Satisfaction guaranteed

SEND CHECK OR MONEY ORDER TO
spencer gifts
OF
ATLANTIC CITY, N. J.

48

Human Interest

Washington Kicks Off National March of Dimes Campaign For Infantile Paralysis

The goal of the national campaign is to raise $30 million.

On hand to get the drive rolling is Margaret Truman pictured with March Of Dimes poster boy Terry Tulos, 3-year old polio victim.

Terry is from Mississippi and drops his dime in the Mississippi jar while Margaret drops her coins in the Missouri jar.

Little Terry receives a very warm reception from President Truman.

The President looks forward to a future when these children will be free of the handicap of braces.

1948 One Million PHILADELPHIANS LINE UP TO SEE THE ANNUAL MUMMERS DAY PARADE

This yearly gay pageant thrills the citizens of Ben Franklin's hometown.

One of the 17 marching string bands adds more excitement to the festivities with their dazzling plumes and brilliantly colored satin Indian costumes.

Elaborately costumed marchers put on a spectacular show of glitter and sparkle complete with female impersonators all in a friendly competition for a long list of prizes.

Miss Inflation is on hand for this big 5 1/2 hour blowout tribute to his majesty, King Momus.

A little clown protection from the light rain for a youthful contestant.

Everyone joins in the carnival spirit.

51

1948

PARADOGS LEAP IN AIR RESCUE

S.O.S. A plane is down in icy wastes of Labrador.

Husky sled dogs are part of "Operation Paradog" and are being used to rescue the downed plane.

The dogs are parachuted and readied for their jump.

From 500 feet altitude, the Paradogs all make their jumps within seconds of each other.

The dogs are harnessed to the sled and begin their rescue trek.

The wrecked plane is located and it's a happy bunch of men who greet their rescuers.

A crash casualty is placed on the sled for a trip to an emergency airstrip where an ambulance is waiting.

WHAT A YEAR IT WAS!

TIME'S MAN OF THE YEAR:
Harry S. Truman

President Truman's
Board Of Foreign Scholarships
Announces First Fulbright Act Scholarships After Rhodes Scholar Senator J. William Fulbright Persuades Congress To Swap The $140 Million In World War II Surplus Rusting Away In Europe For Scholarships.

President Truman Proposes Free Two-Year Community Colleges.

SELECTIVE SERVICE ACT CONTINUES MILITARY DRAFT.

President Truman Ends Army Segregation And Calls For A Fair Employment Policy In Civil Service Ranks.

President Truman Signs The Draft Act Requiring Men From Ages 19-25 To Serve In The Military For Twenty-One Months. 25-Year Olds Register For Second Peacetime Draft.

President Truman Orders The Armed Forces To Begin Integration.

WHAT A YEAR IT WAS!

1948

Research keeps
B.F. Goodrich
FIRST IN RUBBER

Typical example: user's experience with B. F. Goodrich tires

THE smiling man on the right in the picture above is Curtis Corn of Roswell, New Mexico. He and a partner own the 201 Taxi Company and operate a fleet of 16 cabs over a 100-mile radius in New Mexico.

Mr. Corn says his B. F. Goodrich Silvertowns outwear any other tires he has ever owned—including prewar tires. Mr. Corn had a good chance to compare brands during the tire shortage when he used whatever tires he could get. B. F. Goodrich tires outperformed them all.

Here are two examples of B. F. Goodrich tire service from fleet records:

One pair of Silvertowns gave 49,896 miles of continuous, trouble-free service before being removed. And Mr. Corn adds that these casings still looked good for 2,000 *more* miles.

Another pair of B. F. Goodrich tires traveled 42,000 miles on one of the cabs before it was removed and Durecapped. These tires are back in service now.

Experiences like this are common. Hundreds of other enthusiastic B. F. Goodrich owners report outstanding mileages too. B. F. Goodrich tires go farther because tread wear is more uniform. This tread puts a bigger footprint on the road and makes every inch of rubber take its fair share of the load. The tire body has more and stronger cords in it—and a double breaker strip for protection against shocks.

If you need tires, see your B. F. Goodrich dealer today. You'll be surprised what your old tires are worth on a trade-in. If you don't know the address, look under *Tires* in the yellow pages of your phone book. The B. F. Goodrich Company, Akron, Ohio.

B.F. Goodrich
FIRST IN RUBBER

200 SCULPTORS COMPETE IN A SNOWMAN CONTEST HELD IN NEW YORK'S CENTRAL PARK

Snow Angel

Snow Bunny   *Frosty The Friendly Cop*

Salute To Leap Year

This likeness of Babe Ruth wins first prize.

Creator of the Babe Ruth sculpture, Ralph Parton, collects his trophy.

1948

Amsterdam Is The Site Of The First Assembly Of The World Council Of Churches With Roman Catholic And Russian Orthodox Churches Boycotting.

World Jewish Congress Meets In Montreux, Switzerland.

Belgium Grants Women Right To Vote.

THE DEUTSCHE MARK IS ESTABLISHED IN WEST GERMANY.

Captured by American troops in 1918, German born "Kaiser" celebrates his 31st birthday, making him the oldest living homing pigeon in history.

WESTERN EUROPE'S LARGEST DAM OPENS ON RHONE.

THE EARTH ALMOST MOVED FOR HIM
After four years of sleeping on a lumpy mattress, a Frenchman in Angers, France finally rips it open to discover an unexploded German booby-trap mine.

The U.N. General Assembly Meets For The First Time At Flushing Meadow, New York Auditorium.

U.N.'s World Health Organization Begins Operations.

Bread Rationing Ends In Great Britain.

Britain Passes National Health Services Act Offering Free "Cradle To Grave" Medical Care.

Great Britain's House Of Commons Suspends Death Penalty For Five Years.

Sunderland, England Is Site Of World's First Movable-Span Bridge Of Structural Aluminum Constructed Over The River Wear.

Paul Hoffman Appointed Director Of European Relief Program.

U.S. ANNOUNCES STARVATION WORLD'S BIGGEST PROBLEM.

Million And A Half Germans Strike Against Food Administration In American And British Zones.

World Health Assembly Holds First Meeting In Geneva.

1948

Referring To The A-Bomb As "Human Mind's Most Terrible Invention," Pope Pius Asks For A Ban.

The Vatican Announces Excommunication Of All People Involved In The Arrest Of Cardinal Mindszenty.

Princess Elizabeth Gives Birth To Future Heir To British Throne And Four Weeks Later Announces His Name: His Royal Highness Prince Charles Philip Arthur George Of Edinburgh.

King George VI And Queen Elizabeth Lead Royal Procession In Berkshire, England Marking 600th Anniversary Of The Most Noble Order Of The Garter.

Honorary Academician Extraordinary Bestowed Upon Winston Churchill.

Former Under Secretary Of State, Dean Acheson, Goes Back Into Private Law Practice At An Annual Salary Of $100,000.

SUFFRAGE MOVEMENT HONORED WITH A LICKING

The U.S. Post Office Pays Tribute To The Suffrage Movement By Issuing A Stamp Called "100 Years Of Progress Of Women" Including Images Of Elizabeth Stanton, Carrie C. Catt and Lucretia Mott.

Holland's Queen Wilhelmina, 68 **Abdicates Dutch Throne In Favor Of Daughter Juliana, 39, Ending Her 50 Year Reign.**

Aimee Semple McPherson's Foursquare Gospel Church Founded In 1922 Celebrates Its 25th Anniversary.

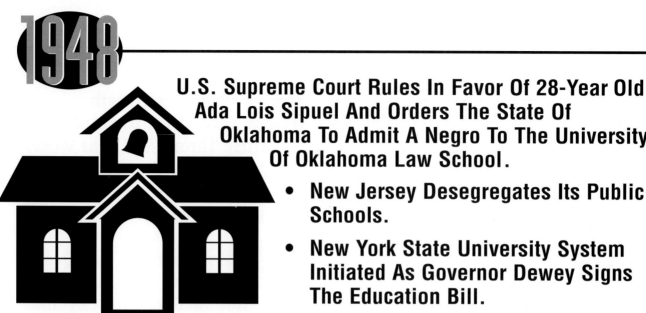

1948

U.S. Supreme Court Rules In Favor Of 28-Year Old Ada Lois Sipuel And Orders The State Of Oklahoma To Admit A Negro To The University Of Oklahoma Law School.

- **New Jersey Desegregates Its Public Schools.**

- **New York State University System Initiated As Governor Dewey Signs The Education Bill.**

The U.S. Passes Federal Rent Control Bill.

Religious Instruction In Public School Ruled Unconstitutional By Supreme Court.

In North Carolina, under a government supported program for a well-balanced lunch, for 5 cents children receive black-eyed peas, eggs, cheese, potatoes, milk, a biscuit and a tangerine.

U.S. Supreme Court Bans Agreements Preventing Negroes From Owning Real Estate.

Nationwide Gallop Poll Shows That 49% Of Americans Favor Racial Integration In Public Transportation While 42% Favor Segregation With The Percentage Rising To 84% In The South.

SOME KIND OF FLYING
Giant Flying Boat "CAROLINE MARS" Lands In Chicago After Nonstop Flight From Honolulu In Record-Breaking Time Of 24 Hours, 9 Minutes.

To Celebrate The Opening Of New York International Airport At Idlewild, Three B-29's Complete First Nonstop Roundtrip Flight Between New York City And Los Angeles, California.

WHAT A YEAR IT WAS!

In An Effort To Help Berlin's Children Lose Their Wartime Fear Of Planes, USAF Lt. Gail Halvorson Drops Candy From His Plane And Is Dubbed the "Candy Bomber."

Two American FJ-1 Fury Fighters Make The First Jet Plane Landing On An Aircraft Carrier Off The Coast Of California.

Six Royal Air Force de Havilland Vampires Land In Nova Scotia After Completing First Jet Crossing Of The Atlantic. 16 U.S. Air Force Shooting Stars Make The Crossing From West To East.

"Kitty Hawk"

Wright Brothers' Plane Finds Permanent Home At Washington's Smithsonian Institute.

COME FLY WITH ME

THE UNITED STATES BEGINS AIR PARCEL SERVICE WITH EUROPE, AFRICA, SOUTH AMERICA AND THE PACIFIC FOLLOWED BY THE U.S. POST OFFICE OFFERING THE SAME SERVICE FOR DOMESTIC USE.

President Truman Approves Airports In Anchorage And Fairbanks.

President Truman Dedicates New York's Idlewild International Airport, The World's Largest Commercial Airport.

Captain Cunningham Sets World Altitude Record Of 59,446 Feet In A de Havilland Airplane.

On A Propeller-Driven Plane, Air France Completes The First Non-Stop Commercial Flight Between Paris And New York In 16 Hours, 1 Minute.

1948

ARE YOU NOW OR HAVE YOU EVER BEEN...

Testifying Before The House Un-American Activities Committee, Whittaker Chambers, Former Communist Spy And Currently A Time Magazine Editor, Accuses Former Top State Department Official Alger Hiss Of Passing Him Secret Government Papers, "The Pumpkin Papers," In The 1930's. Among Other Prominent People Being Accused Are Harry Dexter White, Former Assistant Secretary Of The Treasury And Lauchlin Currie, Both Out Of The Roosevelt Administration. All The Accused Have Denied The Charges.

HUAC Calls For Ouster Of Attorney General Tom Clark If He Refuses To Prosecute Alleged Spies.

Charlie Chaplin Called Before HUAC.

President Truman Denounces The "Spy Hunts" Calling Them A "Red Herring" Designed To Divert Attention Away From His Efforts To Push Through Legislation To Help Curb Inflation.

President Truman Attacks HUAC Calling It "More Un-American Than Those It Investigates."

Moscow Ousts NBC Reporter Robert Magidoff Claiming He's A Spy.

Following A Year-Long Investigation, A Special Federal Grand Jury Indicts 12 High-Ranking Communists On Conspiracy To Overthrow The United States Government Including William Z. Foster, Party Chairman and Benjamin Davis, A New York City Councilman.

Passings

Boys Town for delinquent youths founder **Father Flanagan**, whose life story won an Academy Award for Spencer Tracy in the film "BOYS TOWN," dies at 61.

Anna Jarvis, creator of Mother's Day to honor her own mother, dies at age 84, a spinster.

Philanthropist, social leader and widow of President Theodore Roosevelt, **Edith Kermit Carow Roosevelt** dies at age 87.

E. Eastman Irvine, journalist and editor of the "WORLD ALMANAC," dies at age 65.

SET 'EM UP JOE...
AT LONG LAST

Prohibition Repealed In Kansas After 68 Dry Years.

Ten Inmates Of The Iowa State Penitentiary Join Alcoholics Anonymous.

The United States Sees An Increased Awareness That Chronic Alcoholism Is A Medical And Social Issue.

All Restrictions Removed On The Liquor Industry By Washington.

HE HAD A HOT TIME IN THE OLD TOWN THAT NIGHT

A New Jersey Jury Awards A Gentleman $2,500 For Injuries Sustained While Dozing In A Paterson Saloon Where A Prankster Gave Him A Hotfoot Setting His Pants On Fire.

I'LL HAVE A COKE ON THE ROCKS WITH A TWIST...

THE ANTI-SALOON LEAGUE OF AMERICA CHANGES ITS NAME TO THE TEMPERANCE LEAGUE OF AMERICA AT ITS ANNUAL MEETING IN PITTSBURGH.

LET'S BE CATTY

Vets at a New York animal hospital report two unusual patients – a cat who was hung-over from lapping up too much eggnog and another feline who would eat only if she was serenaded with harmonica music.

1948

HEAD COUNT

The Census Bureau Estimates Population For Continental United States At 147,280,000.

MATTERS OF LIFE & DEATH

DEATH RATE FOR 1948 EQUALS ALL-TIME LOW ESTABLISHED IN 1946.

Birth Rate Drops 8% Over 1947 But September Sees Second Highest Amount Of Births Since Registration Began In 1915.

TEENAGE OUTLOOK

Teenage optimism about the future and high morale cross socio-economic boundaries although they are not as optimistic today as they were during the dark days of World War II.

OLDER WORKERS GAIN NEW RESPECT IN INDUSTRY

The New York State Joint Legislative Committee On Problems Of The Aging Sends Questionnaires To 1,000 Employers And Find Attitudes Toward Hiring Older Workers Is Changing As Follows:

1. Three out of four employers believe older workers produce as much as younger workers.

2. 80% of the employers believe older workers are as loyal as younger workers.

3. 17% of the employers believe older workers are more loyal and conscientious.

4. 72% of employers believe older employees are absent less.

5. The older worker has more experience which eliminates training time and outside distractions.

Well, Three's Not Such A Crowd

Defying the 54,000,000 to one odds, Mrs. Michael Walker of Syracuse, New York gives birth to her second set of triplets.

Mrs. James H. Elkus, Vice President Of The Pittsburgh Planned Parenthood Clinic, Gives Birth To Triplets.

Gerber Products Sells 2 Million Cans And Jars Of Baby Food Weekly.

In The Save-A-Baby Drive, French Mothers Donate Excess Maternal Milk To A Lactarium For Distribution To Undernourished Babies.

U.S. Census Bureau Reports Record High Employment Of 61 Million.

FARMING IS NO HAYRIDE

The Mayo Clinic Reports That Farmers Are Engaged In One Of The Most Dangerous Occupations With A Disabling Accident Striking One American Farmer Every Minute.

New York- Nation's Most Populous State.
Los Angeles- Largest City In Area, Fourth In Population.

I'LL TAKE MANHATTAN, THE BRONX AND STATEN ISLAND, TOO

Mayor William O'Dwyer Heads A "New York At Work" Parade Celebrating The 50th Anniversary Of Brooklyn, Staten Island And Queens Becoming Part Of New York City.

AS PHONY AS A $10 BILL
New York Flooded With Bogus $10 And $20 Almost Perfect Bills – Biggest Counterfeiting Operation In History Of Country.

Dr. W. A. Anderson,
Professor Of Rural Sociology At Cornell University, Completes A Study Of "Joining Habits" Of New York's Rural Residents And Finds The Following:
1. **Only 1 Out Of 10 People Belongs To More Than Three Organizations At Any One Time.**
2. **Women Are The Greatest Joiners.**
3. **Men Are More Inclined To Sit Home And Read The Paper.**

MEATLESS IN NEW YORK

Disgusted over the all-time high price of meat, New York City housewives stage a protest urging the boycott of sirloin steaks and lamb chops.

According To A Survey Released By New York's Cornell University Americans Are Still "Meat-And-Potato" People With Potatoes Their Number 1 Favorite Vegetable.

No decision is reached in Congress with regard to removing taxes on colored oleomargarine or to reduce retailers' fees.

YOU WANNA BET I'M RIGHT?

Dismissed From His Post As Special Deputy Attorney General 48 Hours Before He Is Scheduled To Appear Before The Middlesex County Grand Jury To Present Important Evidence On Gambling, John J. Winberry Charges That New Jersey Is The National Gambling Capital.

The Associated Press, Worldwide News-Gathering Service, Celebrates Its 100th Birthday At Its Annual Meeting At New York's Waldorf-Astoria Hotel.

LET'S NOT CUT THE FAT

The American Fat Salvage Committee recommends handling fat as follows:
- Save fat to the last drop in the pan
- Store in tins or stone crocks
- Set in cool place
- Cook with saved fats
- Sell left-over fat to your local meat dealer

WHAT A YEAR IT WAS!

TO HAVE AND TO HOLD...
TILL DIVORCE DO US PART.

SIMULATED
"ROMANCE DESIGN"
DIAMOND RINGS

SEND NO MONEY

Latest Statistics Indicate Two Out Of Six Marriages End In Divorce.

The World Experiences A Decline In Marriages And Divorces With A Decrease In U.S. Marriages And Divorces Of 10% And 11% respectively.

A DEGREE IN STAYING

A study published by the University Of Chicago reveals college grads have the lowest divorce rates.

EVEN FREE LOADERS HAVE RIGHTS
THE OREGON STATE SUPREME COURT RULES THAT A HUSBAND CANNOT LEGALLY CHARGE HIS MOTHER-IN-LAW FOR ROOM AND BOARD.

THIS IS FOR THE BIRDS

Mrs. Jeanie R. Gordon of Lawrence, Mass. sued her husband for divorce on the grounds that he threw her pet parrot out the window because the bird snitched on him for coming home late.

Ex-Secretary Of Labor Frances Perkins Declares That It Is "...Absurd, anti-social and uneconomic for a woman to work outside the home unless she can earn $4,000 a year."

WHO YA CALLING UGLY!

26-year old Los Angeles housewife Mary E. Magley wins a divorce from her 56-year old husband on the grounds that he kept pictures of his four ex-wives over the bed and continuously pointed out how ugly she was compared to his former wives.

GOOD OLD BACHELOR DAYS...
GOING, GOING, GONE??

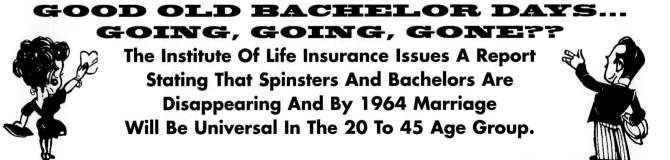

The Institute Of Life Insurance Issues A Report Stating That Spinsters And Bachelors Are Disappearing And By 1964 Marriage Will Be Universal In The 20 To 45 Age Group.

WHAT A YEAR IT WAS!

Construction Is Completed On The "Caronia" The World's Largest Postwar Ocean Liner.

One Million American Homes Now Have Television Sets.

The Franklin-Liberty Bell Replaces The Liberty Walking Half-Dollar By U.S. Mint.

Under Threat Of Ku Klux Klan Retaliation, 400 Registered Negroes In Wrightsville, Georgia Fail To Vote In Johnson County's Primary.

ALL THAT GLITTERS IS GOLD...
The 561 Residents Of Coloma, California Celebrate The 100th Anniversary Of The Discovery Of Gold At Sutter's Mill. A Sparkling Time Was Had By All.

Wagga Wagga *In New South Wales, Australia Is Proclaimed A City.*

 The American Red Cross Inaugurates A Blood Program.

The South American Nutria, A Furry, Aquatic, Nasty Little Wild Rodent-Like Animal With Four Large Orange-Red Front Teeth Capable Of Biting Off A Human Finger In A Single Snap, Have Invaded The U.S. Taking Up Residence From Louisiana To Michigan And Oregon.

Heavy Rains Sweep Through Southern California Bringing Relief From Its Worst Drought In 70 Years.

THE U.S. NATIONAL FOREST SYSTEM, WITH 152 FORESTS IN 40 STATES UNDER ITS CONTROL, CELEBRATES ITS 50TH ANNIVERSARY.

WHAT A YEAR IT WAS!

65

1948

HEY BUDDY, YOU BETTER MOVE THAT TRAIN.

Policemen Issue Traffic Ticket For Overparking To Chicago & Northwestern Railroad Switchman George Skarda Of Omaha Citing Him For Blocking A Crossing With His Train On The City's Main Thoroughfare Plus Eight Other Streets For 30 Minutes.

I'M SURE I PUT MY LIPSTICK IN MY PURSE

Stuffing Her Handbag With 218 Separate Articles Wins Mrs. Harriet Hawk Of Tulsa Oklahoma The Sooner State Business And Professional Women's Club Purse-Cramming Championship. Her Prize: A Flashlight.

EEK, A WOMAN

Dr. Clarence Little Announces That He Developed A Strain Of Mice So Afraid Of Women That The Mice Jump On A Chair When They See A Woman.

Chosen The Oldest Doughnut Dunker In America By The National Dunking Association, 100-Year Old Susan Stewart Has To Decline A Trip To New York Because Of Chronic Indigestion.

A Bill Is Introduced In New York's State Legislature Making It "Unlawful To Drive So Slowly As To Exasperate Other Motorists Into Recklessness."

AND WHAT ARE YOU IN FOR?

A Seattle Federal Jury Finds Man Guilty Of Using A Canceled Five-Cent Stamp.

A Little Rock, Arkansas Bachelor Falls Into Disfavor With The IRS When They Discover He Had Been Claiming His Neighbor's Wife And Children As Dependents.

NOW YOU SEE HIM, NOW YOU DON'T

U.S. Treasury Agents Arrest Income Tax Expert, Vincent J. Cannara Of Bloomfield, New Jersey On Grounds That After Advising His Clients To Take Big Deductions And Collecting His Fees, He Signed Their Income Tax Forms As "Advisor" With Disappearing Ink.

Tho april showers may come your way...

Waiting For The World Tidal Wave He Expects In 1952, William "Noah" Greenwood Builds His Second Ark Near Olympia, Washington Stocking It With 27 Swords, Suit Of Armor, Two Tomahawks, A Cat And A Hat That Belonged To Annie Oakley.

66

WHAT A YEAR IT WAS!

AND TOP CAT AWARD GOES TO...

At The 32nd Championship Show Of The Empire Cat Club Held In New York's McAlphin Hotel The "Best Champion" Award Goes To "Lavender Liberty," A Blue Male Persian. Everyone Thought He Was The Cat's Meow!

OPERATION HEAD START

Falling short a few inches needed to reach the 5'6" requirement to become a policeman, a young applicant plastered his long hair over half a coconut shell which was discovered by doctors during his physical exam.

Russian Teacher Oksana Kosenkina Survives Leap From Third Floor Of Soviet Consulate Stating That She Jumped To Avoid Returning To Russia.

I COULD HAVE DANCED ALL NIGHT—OR THE TURKEY DOES THE TROT

Hoping To Win Themselves A Beautiful Wife, Wild Turkey Gobblers Strut Their Stuff In An Elaborate Mating Dance Trying To Impress The Aloof, But Flirtatious Hens.

HE'S TIED ONE ON

Suggesting That The Europeans Could Use Old Neckties, Harvey W. Morley, Publisher Of The Angola, Indiana "Herald," Receives 20,000 Ties From His Readers.

You Can't Leave 'Till You Clean Your Plate...And Everyone Else's

28 Lunch-Time Customers Are Imprisoned At A Brass Rail Eatery For 35 Minutes By A.F.L. Restaurant Workers Trying A New Strike Technique.

Officials Of The Chicago City Hall Announce That Elevator Operators Are No Longer Allowed To Refer To Some Of The Departments By Their Nicknames As Follows:

	NICKNAME
2nd Floor Criminal Division	"Ball And Chain"
10th Floor Divorce Court	"War Department"
16th Floor Adoption	"Baby Farm"
17th Floor Probate Court	"The Morgue"

WHAT A YEAR IT WAS!

NEW WORDS &

AUREOMYCIN
An antibiotic related to streptomycin and used when streptomycin and penicillin are ineffective.

ECA
European Cooperation Administration (The Marshall Plan).

FAX
Short for facsimile newspaper, one distributed by means of radio waves.

COLD WAR
Phrase coined by Bernard Baruch meaning a conflict carried on by methods short of overt military action and without breaking diplomatic relations.

INTELEX
International Telephone And Telegraph's electronic device for making railroad and airplane reservations in less than a minute.

ISRAEL
The new Jewish Republic in Palestine, proclaimed a state May 14, 1948.

ISRAELI
Of or pertaining to the State of Israel. A citizen of Israel.

CREEPING WAR
War conducted covertly by means of chemicals, germs and electronic devices.

CYBERNETICS
Norbert Wiener coins the word which means the study of information theory.

JOGGING
A popular form of exercise in which the participant runs at a leisurely, easy pace.

DIXIECRAT
Southern Democrats who oppose President Truman's Civil Rights Program.

EXPRESSIONS

LP
Trademark of Columbia Records to describe its Long Playing microgroove record.

MICROGROOVE
Pertaining to a phonograph record with very small grooves.

NUCLEAR FUEL
A radioactive substance such as uranium or plutonium.

PARASITE FIGHTER, PARASITE PLANE
A small plane that operates from a mother plane.

PINTO MAN
A prehistoric man thought to have lived in California 3,000 to 15,000 years ago.

RE-PRINT
A re-release or second release of a motion picture.

SEMIDOCUMENTARY
A partly factual film.

SOUTHCRAT
States' Rights Democrat

TELE
Short for television

TRANSISTOR
Device which takes over most of the functions of the vacuum tube.

TRUMANITE, TRUMANCRAT
Supporter of President Harry S. Truman.

TV
Abbreviation for television.

UNIVAC
Universal Automatic Computer.

A benevolent little imaginary pear-shaped animal able to supply most of mankind's needs created by cartoonist, Al Capp.

XEROGRAPHY
The electronic reproduction of printed material, a process invented by Chester F. Carlson.

1948

360,000 Soft-Coal Workers Go On Strike For $100 Monthly In Retirement Benefits To Begin At Age 62.

In Protest Against Government Decrees, 400,000 French Miners Go On Strike.

Nearly 400,000 United Mine Workers Of America Stop Work.

AMERICA'S FAVORITE DRINKING HABITS

1. Coffee
2. Tea
3. Beer
4. Soft Drinks
5. Hard Liquor

President Truman Authorizes The Federal Government To Seize The Railroads To Avert Scheduled Strike.

HERE COMES THAT HIGH C

Stevens Institute Of Technology's Professor Harold Burris-Meyer Claims That The Reason People Like To Sing In The Bathtub Is Because Their Voices Sound Better To Them In A Small Reverberant Room Which Creates A Satisfying "Acoustic Envelope."

THE ORIGINAL "SOAPS"
Launderettes Become Gathering Places For Women To Do Their Wash And Exchange Gossip.

MISS AMERICA
BeBe Shopp, Minnesota

A Nevada Court Declares Prostitution Legal In Reno.

The Bikini Arrives On American Beaches.

WHAT'S

**"LITTLE AUDREY"
And "REX MORGAN, M.D."
Make Their Respective Comic
Book And Comic Strip Debuts.**

**Walt Kelly's "POGO"
Debuts In The New York Star.**

SUPERMAN

SHMOOZING WITH THE SHMOOS

SUPPOSED TO DO NOW?
Fifty Cities Ban Comic Books Dealing With Crime Or Sex.

Cartoonist Al Capp's Sweet Shmoos Sweep The Country As They Become The Latest Fad.

THIS IS NO JOKING MATTER

IN AN EFFORT TO CONTROL THE GROWING CRITICISM, A NUMBER OF COMIC-BOOK PUBLISHERS FORM THE ASSOCIATION OF COMICS MAGAZINE PUBLISHERS TO TRY TO ESTABLISH A CODE OF STANDARDS FOR THE INDUSTRY TO CIRCUMVENT OUTSIDE CENSORSHIP BUT FAIL IN THEIR EFFORTS TO GET THE COOPERATION OF THE OTHER COMIC-BOOK PUBLISHERS.

New York Supreme Court Invalidates Comic Book Ban.

DONALD DUCK DUCKED BY VENEZUELA

Claiming Donald's Dog "Bolivar" Is An Insult To Venezuela's National Hero, The Venezuelan Motion Picture Workers Union Vow To Ban Walt Disney's Cartoons Until The Dog Gets A Name Change. Disney Capitulates And Deletes Old Bolivar From Its Comic Strips.

. . . and when placed between book covers, The Shmoo makes delicious reading

AND WHY NOT? After all, Shmoos are good for EVERYTHING. Fried, a Shmoo tastes like chicken. Broiled, like prime steak. It gives Grade A milk (in bottles) and pure creamery butter (wrapped in paper). When you eye a Shmoo hungrily, it drops dead of sheer joy. The hide makes the finest leather —or cloth, depending on how thick you slice it. And there are NO BONES.

The definitive book of The Shmoo is now ready. It contains much important and hitherto unrevealed data on this lovable little creature, plus the entire Shmoo continuity from Li'l Abner, plus a preface by Al Capp. Put it in a gift wrapping, and The Shmoo makes a wonderful Christmas present!

THE LIFE AND TIMES OF
THE SHMOO
by Al Capp

On Sale at All Booksellers, Naturherly. Price $1
SIMON AND SCHUSTER, PUBLISHERS

WHAT A YEAR IT WAS!

71

Fragments Of THOUSAND AND ONE NIGHTS, Thought To Be The Oldest Paper Book In Existence Dating Back To A.D. 800-1,000, Is Discovered By Scholar At University Of Chicago.

THE KINSEY REPORT

✓ Alfred C. Kinsey Writes **"Sexual Behavior In The Human Males"** Which Reports The Prevalence Of Sexual Problems And Indicates That 85% Of Married Men Have Had Premarital Sex And 50% Have Been Unfaithful.

The Supreme Court Upholds The Obscenity Ban On Edmund Wilson's "Hecate County."

U.S. Supreme Court Overturns New York State Law Barring Sale Of Books Of Lust, Crime And Bloodshed.

DID YOU HEAR THE ONE ABOUT...

When asked to explain why in the world he would steal a police car, a Brooklyn man replies that he likes the two-tone colors.

Union Allowed To Print Political Views According To The U.S. Supreme Court.

The Voice Of America Becomes Permanent Agency Of The State Department.

The Philadelphia Inquirer Becomes First U.S. Newspaper To Broadcast Facsimile Editions.

The Periodicals UNITED STATES NEWS And WORLD REPORT Merge As U.S. NEWS AND WORLD REPORT.

IN PRINT IN PRINT IN

68% OF AMERICANS BELIEVE IN AN AFTERLIFE.

DO YOU BELIEVE IN GOD?
A GOD POLL

COUNTRY	YES	NO
BRAZIL	96%	3%
AUSTRALIA	95%	5%
CANADA	95%	2%
UNITED STATES	94%	3%
NORWAY	84%	7%
FINLAND	83%	5%
HOLLAND	80%	14%
SWEDEN	80%	8%
DENMARK	80%	9%
FRANCE	66%	20%

Don't Forget To Take Out The Used Food Bags, Honey???

The City of Waterbury, Connecticut changes job title from "Supervisor of Garbage Disposal" to "Superintendent of Used Food Collection" at new supervisor's insistence.

HOWLING AT THE MOON OR... THE MOON MADE ME DO IT, YOUR HONOR

Following the sentencing of John Henry Cole to 15 years in prison, the London press took another look at the moon's influences on human behavior since Mr. Cole's crimes of assaults on women and robbery were all committed during the new moon phase.

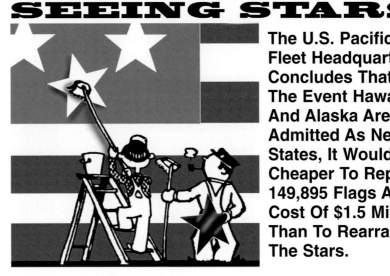

NEW YORK'S TROOP 111

Of The Boy Scouts Of America Is Installed With 10 New Members, All Blind Or Partially Sighted. Congratulations For This Milestone Event Pour In From Governor Dewey, Bernard Baruch And Hank Greenberg.

SEEING STARS

The U.S. Pacific Fleet Headquarters Concludes That In The Event Hawaii And Alaska Are Admitted As New States, It Would Be Cheaper To Replace 149,895 Flags At A Cost Of $1.5 Million Than To Rearrange The Stars.

WHAT A YEAR IT WAS!

1948

JUST ONE KISS, THEN ONE MORE...

Dr. Dorothy T. Spoerl, Psychologist At The American International College Of Springfield, Mass., Tells Her Students That There Is Nothing "As Wholesome As Good Clean Necking" At The Right Time And The Right Place.

TEENAGE STUDENT CULTURE:

MOST ADMIRED BOYS: STAR ATHLETES

XXX MOST ADMIRED GIRLS: THE MOST POPULAR WITH BOYS

"RODDERS"

FIRST PRODUCT OF THE ATOMIC AGE

5,000 "Hot Rods" Hit The Los Angeles Roads As Teenage Boys Get Swept Up In The Postwar Phenomenon Of Buying Old Cars And Turning Them Into "Hopped Up Heaps."

WANNA GO STEADY?

The Once Coveted Fraternity Pin Signifying "Going Steady" Has Been Replaced With His And Her Matching Sweaters Called The "Steady Sweater." So What Do You Tell Your Friends? I Got Sweatered Last Night.

CONVERSATION STARTERS FOR TEENAGE GIRLS:

- Tell Charles about the first time you ever saw him. "It was the first day of school two years ago in History Class. You were wearing a white shirt and red tie."

- Talk about your animals: "My cat has ticks – What do you think I can do about that?"

- Talk about foreign languages: "Are you taking French?" "Have you travelled?"

- Do not plan your sentences or use newest slang expressions frequently.

DATING

Provides Opportunities For Intimacy And Sexual Exploration But Usually Stops At Petting.

KISSING COMES BACK TO THE BALCONY

Organized To Discourage Necking In Movie Theatres, The Juarez, Mexico Feminine Police Corps. Is Disbanded When Theatre Owners Complain Of A Severe Box-Office Slump.

A GIRL TRIES TO ATTRACT A BOY SUBTLY NEVER LETTING HIM KNOW THAT SHE IS CHASING HIM.

WHO YOU CALLING A SISSY?

According To A Study Done At The Fels Research Institute In Ohio, Girls Relax More Easily Than Boys And Need Less Time To Recover From Stress.

Being A Member Of A Clique Enhances A Girl's Value On The Dating Market Because That Makes Her Part Of A "Leading Crowd."

Due To The Failure Of Embarrassed Teachers To Provide Necessary Instruction Using Pamphlets, Slides And Lectures, Oregon Junior High Schools Offer Coed Classes In Sex Education Using Educational Movies.

I'M NOT FICKLE – JUST WELL ADJUSTED

The American Journal Of Sociology reports that a young man or woman who has "gone steady" with two or three members of the opposite sex (not at the same time, of course) is better adjusted emotionally than the person who has had only one "steady." On the other hand, if you've had more than four steadies, you're just plain fickle.

 **The sleek,** trim lines of the Stetson *Whippet*…and the bold sweep of its bound brim…help to give you that confident, up-and-coming look that says you're "going places." And the *Whippet* is going places, too—it's America's favorite hat! $10.

The STETSON *Whippet*

More people wear Stetson Hats than any other brand. Stetson Hats are made only by John B. Stetson Company and its subsidiary companies in the United States and Canada.

BUSINESS

AMERICAN PRODUCTION OF GOODS REACHES GREATEST PEACETIME RECORD

 U.S. CONSUMER PRICE INDEX REACHES RECORD HIGH OF 173 AGAINST 1935-1939 AVERAGE.

 U.S. TOY INDUSTRY ENJOYS BIGGEST CHRISTMAS IN HISTORY.

 U.S. PLANTS AND FACILITIES EXPERIENCE RECORD NEAR-CAPACITY UTILIZATION.

 FARMERS ENJOY RECORD CROP YIELDS.

THE INDEX OF LEADING ECONOMIC INDICATORS IS ORIGINATED.

THE TISHMAN REALTY AND CONSTRUCTION COMPANY CELEBRATES ITS 50TH ANNIVERSARY WITH RECORD EARNINGS.

Arrests Are Made As 600 Boisterous Pickets From Both The A.F.L. United Financial Employees And A.F.L. Seafarers Unions Block Entrances To The New York Stock And Curb Exchanges.

Boeing Strike Lasts 140 Days Before Settlement Is Reached.

Benjamin Franklin's Image Appears On First New Half Dollar Coin Issued By U.S. Treasury Since 1916.

1948

- **V**ehicle Production Hits Over 5,000,000 In The Second Greatest Production Year In The Industry.

- **C**hrysler Grants Workers Wage Increase Of 13 Cents Per Hour Ending A 17-Day Strike.

- **H**onda Technical Research Institute Incorporates As The Honda Motor Company.

- **H**udson Automobile Designer Frank Spring Unveils New Look For Postwar American Cars.

- **U**niversal Adoption Of Automatic Transmission Almost Complete In The U.S.

- **S**tudebaker And Hudson Capture A Record-Breaking 18% Of The Domestic Automobile Market.

- **U.S.** Automobile Manufacturers Claim Expansion Of Life Span Of Cars From 6.5 Years To 13.4 Years.

- **P**reston Tucker Announces The "Tucker Torpedo" Is The New American Dream Car.

- **G**eneral Motors Produces New High-Compression V-8 Engine Capable Of Offering More Horsepower Than Any Other Previous Engine With Enough Efficiency To Power New Frills Such As Power Brakes, Power Steering, Power Seats And Air Conditioning.

1948 Lincoln

WHAT A YEAR IT WAS!

It's America's favorite "take a picture" car!

YOU NEVER SAW A CAR LIKE the new Studebaker for getting itself included in "special occasion" family snapshots.

It's such a naturally photogenic car, in fact, we always illustrate it with color camera pictures ourselves.

New grace of line is the secret of the new Studebaker's eye appeal. It's the most refreshing change in car design in years.

All America loves this new look that Studebaker originated! Those low-swung dreamlines are today's top fashion in cars.

You find every new Studebaker a thrill car in riding comfort and handling ease, too —and in panoramic new visibility!

Body styles include Champion and Commander convertibles, sedans, coupes —a special extra-long-wheelbase Land Cruiser!

STUDEBAKER

First in style…first in vision…first by far with a postwar car

The First American-Built Electric Locomotive Is Tested By The General Electric And American Locomotive Companies.

Scandinavian Airlines Is Formed As Civil Aviation Companies Of Denmark, Norway And Sweden Combine Their Operations Into A Single Unit.

Ned Orbach Opens His Orbach's In The "Miracle Mile" Section Of Los Angeles.

Baskin-Robbins Chain Begins.

Northwest Airlines Opens Hawaii Service.

Capable Of Assembling A Fully-Finished House In Six Days Complete With Shrubs And Concrete Walks For $5,750, National Homes Becomes Popular Builder Of Pre-fabricated Houses.

Three thrilling moments

FOR A BRAND NEW MOTHER

1. When **you** see your new baby for the first time...and your new life as a mother begins... that's your proudest moment.

2. When the **family** sees baby, you're thrilled to present the newest, most precious member to those beaming relatives.

3. When the **world** sees baby in his new

Thayer FOLDING COACH

THAT'S a thrilling moment indeed, the first time you parade your little king or queen down the avenue! A lovely baby in a *lovely carriage* will turn all heads. The new THAYER FOLDING COACH is America's most beautiful infant vehicle, with its gleaming aluminum chassis and its flexible plastic body in your choice of glowing colors. And of course THAYER is a by-word for baby comfort and safety. Baby rides in luxurious upholstery, on a shock-proof, sway-proof chassis. "Feather-Touch"

Back Rest adjusts instantly to three positions. Aluminum push handle adjusts to mother's height. Then there are safety brakes with Non-Tip stand, big bicycle-type wheels with self-oiling, squeak-proof bearings and semi-pneumatic tires ... but see for yourself when you inspect the new THAYER at your favorite store! Or send 10 cents for your copy of "PRIMER FOR PARENTS" to Thayer, Inc., Dept. LM2, Gardner, Mass. (In Canada, address Bruce Stauffer & Co., Ltd., Montreal 25).

Carriages • Strollers • Toddlers • Hi-Chairs • Cribs • Training Seats • Pres-Toe-Pens

Thayer IS THE GLAMOUR NAME IN JUVENILE PRODUCTS.

Average Salaries Per Year

Average	$ 2,933.00
Electrical Employees	3,223.00
Medical Employees	1,918.00
Motion Picture Employees	2,964.00
Public Schoolteachers	2,538.00
Railroad Employees	3,611.00
Telegraph Employees	2,776.00

Average Yearly Expenses

Clothing	$ 114.57
Food	369.64
Automobile	105.71
Furniture	19.09
Utilities	45.01
Physicians	16.37
Dentists	5.46
Recreation	66.15

Cruise
New York to Bombay, 38 days ... $ 660.00

Airline Reservations
LaGuardia to:

Los Angeles	99.00
San Francisco	88.00
Miami	50.00
Phoenix	99.00

Passings

John Robert Gregg, inventor of the Gregg shorthand system used around the world, dies at age 80.

Ingersoll watch company co-founder **Henry Ingersoll** dies after being hit by a car at age 82.

George Johnson, liberal president of the second largest shoe manufacturer in the U.S., and cause of Lestershire, New York's name change to Johnson City, dies at age 91.

Josiah Lilly, chairman of the board of Eli Lilly and Company, founded by his father, dies at age 87.

Co-founder of publishing giant McGraw-Hill, publisher **James McGraw** dies at age 87.

Inventor of the Nash automobile, Nash-Kelvinator chairman of the board and veteran of such venerable car companies as Buick and General Motors, **Charles Nash** dies at age 84.

Charles Nash

Wilhelm von Opel, German automobile maker known as the "Henry Ford of Germany" and former member of the Nazi party, dies in Germany at age 76.

Alvah Curtis Roebuck, co-founder of Sears, Roebuck & Co., dies at age 84.

Half of the Wright Brothers team—aviation pioneers and airplane inventors—**Orville Wright**, owner of Aircraft Pilot Certificate #1, dies at age 76.

Orville Wright

1948

this was the price that was

Adding Machine	$ 120.00
Apples, lb.	.13
Aqua Velva	.50
Athletic Supporter	1.50-2.00
Bra	1.25-3.95
Bracelet, charm	4.50
Butter, lb.	.90

Candy Corn	$ .10
Candy, Jujyfruits	.05
Candy, after dinner mints	.10
Car, Buick Roadmaster	2,900.00
Car, DeSoto Convertible	2,500.00
Car, Nash	3,100.00
Car, Packard	4,300.00
Car, Rolls Royce	18,500.00

Cheese, lb.	$ .67
Chocolates, Whitman's, lb.	2.00
Cigars	.15-.35
Clock Radio	29.95
Coffee, lb.	.53
Coat, men's	70.00
Coca-Cola	.05
Coffee, lb.	.53
Diamond, 1 carat	600.00-1185.00
Eggs, doz.	.72
Electric Broom	44.95
Electric Train Set	39.75
Face Powder	1.00
Faucet	.39
Flashlight	1.65-1.95
Flatware	23.00

Flowers, pkg. Begonias	$ .50
Girdle	5.50-10.95
Glycerine tablets	.10
Golf Balls, doz.	4.94
Golf Clubs, irons	31.44-49.94
Hair Tonic	.25
Home Hair Permanent	1.50-2.75
Humidifier	2.50
Juicer, manual	7.95
Laxative, Ex-lax	.10
Light Bulb, 40/60 watt	.12
Lighter, windproof	6.00-8.25
Lipstick	1.00-1.50
Magazine, Life-1 yr sub.	6.00
Magazine, Sat. Eve. Post	.15
Magazine, Vogue	.50
Margarine	.30-.40

Milk, qt	$ .22
Muff	1.95-2.50
Paint Sprayer, electric	29.95
Pen Set	12.50
Perfume	1.75-3.00
Pipe, tobacco	1.50
Potato Baker/Bun Warmer	3.00
Powder Compact	1.00-1.50
Rain Coat, men's	14.75-18.50

REAL ESTATE

4-story English basement dwelling w/garden sells for $43,000.

6-story apartment is assessed at $52,000.

6-story apartment house with 24 apartments and a store is assessed at $17,000.

Razors, 10 pack	$ 1.00
Rice, lb	.21
Ring, engagement	375.00
Ring, wedding	200.00
Robe, men's	17.50
Robe, women's	21.95
Rouge	.50
Shaver, electric	16.50
Shoes, women's pumps	10.95-12.95
Socks, wool	1.65-5.00
Socks, women's	.39-.59
Stapler	2.20
Stockings, nylon	1.65
Sugar, lb	.09
Swim Trunks, men's	4.95
Tape, cellophane	.25

Television	$ 445.00
Tie, men's	1.50
Tobacco, chewing	.25
Tobacco, pipe	.15
Tweezers	.50
Undershirt	.85
Watch Band, oval shaped	1.00
Windshield Wiper Blades	.50
Yarn, oz	.35

See how much *more* food the Space Maker keeps under refrigeration!

In the picture on the left above, you see a conventional 6-cubic-foot refrigerator. In front of it is all the food it can possibly hold in its refrigerated storage space. On the right is the 8-cubic-foot General Electric Space Maker. Just *look* how much food it can keep under refrigeration—*a full third more!* And though it seems incredible, the Space Maker fits in almost exactly the same kitchen floor space as an old-style six-cubic-foot refrigerator!

THE beautiful new 1948 General Electric Space Maker Refrigerator *not only* offers you unmatched dependability and one-third more *refrigerated* storage space. . . . The Space Maker Refrigerator has all these outstanding *additional* advantages:

Butter Conditioner—keeps butter constantly at the right spreading temperature.

Big Freezing Compartment—holds 24 packages of frozen food, plus 4 ice trays.

Drawers 6 Inches Deep—hold standing roasts and two-thirds bushel of fruits and vegetables under refrigeration.

Bottle Storage Space—holds 12 square, quart-size milk bottles, also tallest bottles.

Sliding "Hostess" Shelf—convenient for chilling both desserts and salads. Can be removed and used as a serving tray.

5-Year Protection Plan—included in the price, and accompanying every G-E Refrigerator, is a 5-Year Protection Plan. This plan consists of a one-year warranty on the complete refrigerator, plus additional 4-year protection on the sealed-in refrigerating system.

See them at your retailer's NOW!

You can see these gleaming white Space Maker Refrigerators at your retailer's *today!* He can show you a choice of three 8-cubic-foot models and two 10-cubic-foot models. General Electric Company, Bridgeport 2, Connecticut.

Space Maker Refrigerators

GENERAL ⊛ ELECTRIC

⅓ More Refrigerated Food Storage In The Same Kitchen Floor Space!

Great new 1948 General Electric Space Maker Refrigerator

Backed by an unequalled record for dependable service

More than 1,700,000 G-E Refrigerators in service 10 years or longer!

Like all G-E Refrigerators, the Space Maker is equipped with the famous sealed-in refrigerating system. This marvelously efficient system, pioneered by General Electric, has an unmatched record for year-in, year-out dependability . . . for smooth, quiet, most economical operation. *And today's system — more efficient than ever — has ⅓ more freezing capacity, makes ice cubes 33⅓ per cent faster, and consumes less current than our latest prewar refrigerators!*

Good things happen over Coffee...

When young love's fondest dreams unfold,
They're more than attic walls can hold—

And coffee's there beside their dreams,
To add its warmth to love's best schemes—

For coffee's hearty zest endears
Good things that happen through the years,

And it belongs where helpmates are
While they're reaching for a star.

*Some say iced,
Some say hot,
But all say it's nice
To get what coffee's got!*

How to make delicious Coffee

Look for this Seal of Recommendation on the coffee maker you buy. It means coffee experts recommend it for getting the most in flavor, clarity and aroma from the coffee you use.
Always keep coffee maker clean.
For each 6 oz. cup of water, use one Standard Measure of coffee. If your store doesn't have the Standard Coffee Measure illustrated, send 10¢ (to cover mailing and packing costs) to Pan-American Coffee Bureau, P. O. Box 78, New York 8, N. Y. You can also get the booklet, "Coffee Brewing". It gives complete directions on how to brew coffee by all brewing methods.

PAN-AMERICAN COFFEE BUREAU
Brazil • Colombia • Costa Rica • Cuba • Dominican Republic • El Salvador • Guatemala • Mexico • Venezuela
With the cooperation of the NATIONAL COFFEE ASSOCIATION

SCIENCE & MEDICINE

FEAR OF SMELLING

According to a study released in the American Journal Of Physical Anthropology, contrary to previously held scientific opinion, chimpanzees have a sharper sense of smell than human beings and will react with fear to an unfamiliar odor.

AND REMEMBER THAT...

Birds of bright feathers are less tasty than their dull-feathered counterparts according to British naturalist, Dr. Hugh B. Cott.

FOLLOW THAT FISH

Goldfish cruise at a speed of about 1 1/7 miles an hour according to research conducted at the University Of Toronto.

FOR LADY FISH ONLY

A 1" minnow, "Mollienisia Formosa" or "Amazon Molly," is causing scientists to scratch their heads as after 12 years of laboratory breeding 8,000 offspring are produced with not one male among them. Who says it's a man's world??

LAUGHING MATTERS

The American Journal Of Psychiatry reports that the use of nitrous oxide or "laughing gas" is being used successfully in the treatment of mental patients by calming them down and in some cases has proven effective in aiding partial recovery.

FRUIT OFF THE VINE IS DEVINE OR MEET ME WITH NO MEAT IN ST. LOUIE, LOUIE

Those of you concerned with the high-cost of meat, be of good cheer as the only animals that live longer than man, the giant tortoises of the Galapagos and Seychelle Islands, are card-carrying vegetarians. The other longest living non-human mammal vegetarian is the elephant followed by our kissing cousins, the great apes with parrots holding the old-age record for vegetarian birds.

THAT'S NO YOLK

The egg white is a richer source of nutritious protein than the yolk according to a professor at Georgetown University.

TWINS, A THING OF THE PAST

According to Professor A.H. Schultz of Johns Hopkins mankind seems to be losing the ability to produce multiple births and the present generation of parents are more likely to parent twins than their great-great-great grandchildren will be.

SCIENCE ON THE VERGE OF PREDICTING SEX OF THE UNBORN BABY

A new blood test is being developed that will effectively predict the sex of unborn babies with 70% to 90% accuracy as early as five months before birth.

★ Doctors encourage close contact with newborn babies by their mothers to develop immediate mother and child relationships.

★ According to a Yale professor, many miscarriages of early pregnancy take place due to an insufficient concentration of thyroid hormone in the blood.

★ A University of Chicago study of 1,000 maternity cases of women 40 to 45 shows them at greater health risk than their younger counterparts.

★ $1.18 million allotted to U.S. and Canadian Universities by the National Foundation for Infantile Paralysis for polio research and training.

★ Studies reveal that women who get out of bed within one to two days after childbirth have a more rapid convalescence and less depression.

TEST TUBE BABIES NEARER THAN YOU THINK

Although up until now test tube babies were a dream of biological romancers and romantic biologists, a first short step has been taken in that direction with the test-tube fertilization of human ova with human spermatozoa as reported at the meeting of the American Association of Anatomists at Madison, Wisconsin by Drs. Miriam F. Menkin and John Rock of Harvard Medical School and the Brookline, Mass. Free Hospital For Women.

AND NOW A WORD FROM THE NEANDERTHALS

Massachusetts defeats birth-control referendum allowing physicians to prescribe contraceptives to married women whose health would be threatened by pregnancy.

First comprehensive program on research into human reproduction begins in the United States. A poll of over 3 million women shows that 97% approve birth-control measures for use by married women.

I THOUGHT I SAW A PURPLE COW— *I DID, I DID!!*

More than 250 scientists gathered at the Alabama Polytechnic Institute are stunned beyond belief as they watch motion pictures of the only purple cow in existence during a conference on the use of atomic substances in agricultural research. The peculiar coloration is ascribed to insufficient copper in its diet.

NOW IF WE COULD JUST FIGURE OUT HOW TO MILK A WHALE...

According to an article appearing in Nature magazine, whale milk contains highly concentrated amounts of ascorbic acid (vitamin C) and double the amount found in cow's milk.

A WINDOW OF OPPORTUNITY

The $1,000 Borden Award goes to Dr. A.F. Schalk for building a window in a cow's stomach for purposes of observing the cow's digestive processes.

Millions of dinosaur skeletons discovered in the Gobi Desert of Mongolia by Russian Paleontologist I.A. Efremov.

In an effort to kill disease-bearing mosquitoes, a recording of a female mosquito humming a love song lures 40,000 males to their death as they fly into an electrified screen in a Cuban swamp.

A new antimalarial drug developed by Columbia University.

British scientists find tsetse fly cure.

YES, BUT WILL IT HIT THE CHARTS

Cornell scientist Professor Paul Kellogg reports that his team has recorded the sound of a moth chewing through fabric and it sounds like someone eating corn flakes.

Swiss chemist Paul Müller comes up with formula for DDT for insect control.

Glass lung tested on dog at the New York Eye And Ear Infirmary.

Commander Finne Ronne reports that Antarctica is a single continent, not two separate islands.

Geologists predict crude oil scarcity by 1958.

• A five-man research team announces the development of a high-dosage shot of penicillin that remains effective for four days.

• New York attacks 250,000 hidden cases of venereal disease with 45 billion units of penicillin and hundreds of radio ads.

• The U.S. Atomic Energy Commission distributes radioactive isotopes for use in cancer treatment and reports successful use of irradiated cobalt in cancer treatment.

• The American Heart Association advises anti-blood clotting drugs significantly reduce deaths from coronary thrombosis.

• Army researchers report that typhoid fever can be cured in three days with new drug called Chloromycetin.

• Antibiotic Aureomycin is developed.

• First international poliomyelitis conference held in New York votes to set up permanent world congress on polio.

• According to the United States Public Health Service, 1948 is second worst year for recorded cases of polio.

• World Health Organization announces development of new process for extracting insulin.

• Lederle Laboratories in New York discovers that vitamin B-12 builds red corpuscles in pernicious anemia sufferers.

• Yale Medical School announces development of rubberized nylon respirator to replace the iron lung.

• Coxsackie B virus also called hand, foot and mouth disease, discovered in upstate New York.

• The New York University post-graduate medical school is founded.

• U.S. Public Health Services disclose new 5-minute procedure to test for diabetes to go nationwide.

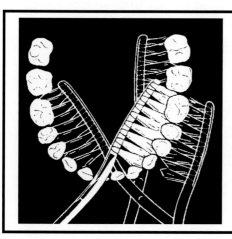

50,000 children get their teeth coated with sodium fluoride in New York City's Fluoridation Program for the prevention of tooth decay.

The American Dental Association announces its opposition to Truman's proposed national health insurance.

American Dental Association study reveals that four out of five or 80.7% of toothbrushes used in American homes are useless or dangerous and recommend frequent replacement.

♥ Some heart disease victims helped by vitamin E.

♥ Heart and circulatory disorders account for 33% of all deaths in the United States.

♥ National Heart Institute is established under the United States Public Service.

• For the first time a new method for using the powerful electron microscope makes it possible to look within blood cells and bacteria.

• Cerebral Palsy clinic for children opens in New York.

• Painless hypodermic injection of penicillin and certain other drugs accomplished by chilling the skin around the injection site.

• Benadryl used successfully by a Navy doctor in the treatment of the common cold.

• Sulfa drugs used successfully in the treatment of meningitis where penicillin and streptomycin fail.

• Tuberculosis leading incapacitating and death-causing disease worldwide.

• Immunologist Bettina Carver develops Rh Hapten to save "RH" babies.

• Stainless steel pin introduced for use in repairing bone fractures.

The Medical Society Of The State Of New York Adopts A Resolution Urging The End Of Racial Discrimination In Admission To The American Medical Association.

THE UNIVERSITY OF CALIFORNIA publishes a report in The Journal Of The American Medical Association stating that people in the lower middle class are most subject to chronic disease and intelligent people tend to have a hard time recovering from sickness.

Rehabilitation centers in the United States and Great Britain place emphasis on the training of speech therapists and the integration of speech therapy into medical care.

MEDICAL AUTHORITIES WARN THAT X-RAY SHOULD NOT BE USED FOR THE REMOVAL OF SUPERFLUOUS HAIR.

ALBERT LASKER AWARDS (for medical research of a pioneering nature)

Vincent du Vigneaud	Basic study of transmethylation and contributions to structure and synthesis of biotin and penicillin.
Selman A. Waksman & Rene J. Dubos	Joint study of antibiotic properties of soil bacteria. Waksman is also honored for the discovery of streptomycin.

WHAT A YEAR IT WAS!

The AMA Meets In St. Louis To Plan Strategies For Raising $3.5 Million To Fight President Truman's National Health Insurance Program.

British Physicians

Vote Overwhelmingly Not To Join Free Medical Service System Set Up By National Health Service Act.

A Shocking Recovery

The American Journal Of Psychiatry reports that a series of electric shock treatments completely cures a young girl of chronic severe stammering.

BROOKINGS INSTITUTE REPORTS THE GENERAL HEALTH OF AMERICANS IS HIGHEST EVER REACHED IN HISTORY AND HIGHER THAN ANY OTHER NATION IN THE WORLD.

PASS THE GUN, PASS THE MASKS, PASS THE TUMS

DR. DAVID ABRAHAMSEN, PSYCHIATRIST AT COLUMBIA UNIVERSITY, CONCLUDES FROM A FOUR-YEAR STUDY THAT 50% OF CRIMINALS SUFFER FROM INDIGESTION TRACED TO FRICTION IN THE HOME WHEN THEY WERE GROWING UP.

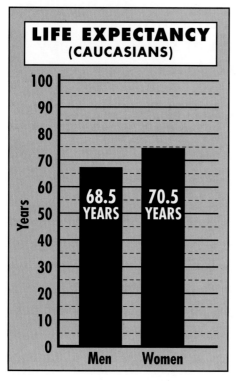

Ultrasonic, high frequency sound waves are being tested as an anesthetic in several clinics while at the same time according to a study at the Wisconsin Psychiatric Institute at Madison, Wisconsin, they can cause epileptic convulsions.

SWEET & BLUE

Hungarian research reports in The Technology Review that saccharin could cause a mood swing as it causes a temporary decrease in the amount of sugar circulating in your blood.

How To Recognize A "Psychopathic" Personality
(Now Ladies, Don't Panic)

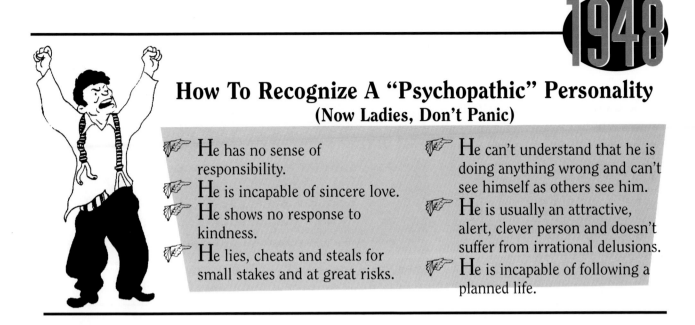

☞ He has no sense of responsibility.

☞ He is incapable of sincere love.

☞ He shows no response to kindness.

☞ He lies, cheats and steals for small stakes and at great risks.

☞ He can't understand that he is doing anything wrong and can't see himself as others see him.

☞ He is usually an attractive, alert, clever person and doesn't suffer from irrational delusions.

☞ He is incapable of following a planned life.

STUDIES OF PRE-SCHOOL CHILDREN REVEAL THAT CONTRARY TO TRADITIONAL BELIEF, BOYS ARE MORE EMOTIONAL THAN GIRLS.

Psychiatry Reaches Peak Of Public Interest Which Brings Insights Into The Prevention And Treatment Of Many Emotional States Of Children.

The Hale Telescope, world's largest telescope (200-inch), dedicated at California Institute Of Technology's observatory on Mount Palomar, 80 miles south of Los Angeles.

SEX & SUICIDE

Although more women than men attempt suicide, more men actually succeed according to a study conducted at the Northwestern University Medical School.

NOBEL PRIZES

MEDICINE & PHYSIOLOGY	PHYSICS	CHEMISTRY
Paul H. Müller (Switzerland)	Lord Patrick M.S. Blackett (Britain)	Arne W.K. Tiselius (Sweden)

Rocket Sled Hurtles 1,000 MPH

A technician from Northrup gets sled ready for an assault on the sonic barrier.

Powered by five rockets *(below left)* and held in place by magnesium slippers *(below middle)*, the Northrup land vehicle will be adapted as an outdoor wind tunnel for testing aircraft flying beyond the speed of sound.

Man's attempts to crack that supersonic barrier lead to some spectacular experiments with this sled topping 1,000 miles per hour.

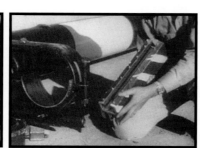

U.S. Navy Rocket Sets New Record For U.S. Rocket Missiles As It Reaches Speed Of 3,000 M.P.H. And Altitude Of 78 Miles In Tests At White Sands, New Mexico.

Captain Charles Yeager Breaks The Sound Barrier In A Rocket-Powered Bell X-1 At 35,000 Feet.

New Liquid Hydrogen Fuel For Rockets Is Announced By H.L. Johnson Who Says It Will "Send Men To The Moon."

The U.S. Army Signal Corp. Announces An Unmanned Sounding Balloon Has Broken The Altitude Record For Any Man-Made Object Except Rockets Rising A Record 26 Miles Or 140,000 Feet.

Unofficial Reports Reveal That The Douglas D-558 Skyrocket Clocked At The Speed Of Sound—650 MPH At An Altitude Of 35,000 Feet.

IS THERE LIFE ON MARS?

1948

Lacking space ships, astronomers take advantage of a favorable alignment for viewing Mars through an 82-inch telescope set up in McDonald's Observatory atop Mount Locke in the Davis Mountains of Texas and made some of the following observations:

1. White polar caps of snow or ice.
2. Red areas that appear to be deserts or rusty rock.
3. Greenish zones that could be vegetation.
4. The atmosphere contains carbon dioxide, oxygen and moisture—all favorable to life.
5. The planet is free from poisonous ammonia and methane.

6. The atmosphere is thin and lacks the gases that filter out the blistering ultra-violet part of sunlight.
7. Nights are freezing—80 degrees below zero at the equator.
8. Green areas could be covered with lichen, a low form of plant life that clings to rocks in many parts of the earth.
9. The planet appears to be too rugged to support other forms of higher plant or animal life including humans.
10. Observance of the "well-engineered canals" thought to bring water from the polar icecaps to irrigate the farms of a civilized Martian community are not consistently visible.
11. Final answers may not come until Mars is visited by a rocketship from Earth.

1948

COFFEE, TEA OR LET'S CIRCLE THE AIRPORT ONE MORE TIME

A new experimental radar operation has been installed at Queens College, Flushing, New York to monitor the skies for airplanes approaching New York airports with the hope that this surveillance will help in speeding up approaches and cut down stacking delays.

The Civil Aeronautics Board rules that all scheduled passenger airlines must be equipped with early warning radar.

First port radar system introduced in Liverpool, England.

Columbia University mineralogist discovers new uranium-bearing ore in Belgian Congo.

The University of California reveals its creation of the first man-made Meson, short-lived particles knocked out of atomic nuclei.

"Nuclear Energy Is Here For Good" travelling exhibition makes first appearance at the American Museum of Natural History in New York.

Mummy Discovered In The Red Pyramid Believed To Be The Remains Of King Snefru Disappears Shortly After Discovery.

A Rainmaking Bag Once The Property Of A 103-Year Old Indian Medicine Man Proves More Effective Than Scientific Rainmakers.

Tight Corsets Thought To Help Cause Stomach Ulcers

WARNINGS ISSUED ABOUT THE DANGERS OF WAX CRAYONS IF INGESTED BY CHILDREN

BREATHE AT YOUR OWN RISK

Polluted Air Responsible For At Least 700 Deaths A Year In Chicago With Other Industrialized American Cities Experiencing Similar Fatalities.

Dav·N·Bed
by INTERNATIONAL

gives you honest-to-goodness living room furniture and a full-size double bed, too!

For the first time — and only in Dav-N-Bed — you can enjoy all these quality features at a new low price

- *pure living room design that never lets anyone suspect you are concealing a bed*
- *the luxurious comfort that only a full-size innerspring mattress can give*
- *matching chair for a handsome living room suite*
- *other styles available, not illustrated*

See Dav-N-Bed at your International dealer's now. See how much more it gives you — and saves you.

Look for this tag on fine STURDILUX furniture by INTERNATIONAL
International's Golden Anniversary — 1898 to 1948

IN FABRICS OF MATCHED

Kleersheen COLORS FROM

THE SHELTON LOOMS

Write us for the name of your nearest International dealer

INTERNATIONAL FURNITURE COMPANY
Makers of living room furniture with KANT SAG and STURDILUX constructions

EXECUTIVE OFFICES: 666 Lake Shore Drive, Chicago 11, Illinois • FACTORIES AT: Rushville, Ind.
Montoursville, Pa. • Madison, Ga. • Bryan, Texas • Cornelia, Ga. • Jacksonville, Texas

Leave your bedding on the bed. Merely raise up and out by the helpful handle. When open, Dav-N-Bed is a full-size double bed with innerspring mattress.

NEW PRODUCTS AND INVENTIONS

Kurlash introduces curler for eyelashes.

Max Factor introduces "Pan-Stik," a foundation that comes in a container similar to lipstick.

West Germany is the manufacturing home to the newly founded **Adidas** athletic shoe.

The **Veg-O-Mat** machine company of New York introduces electric vegetable juice extractor for home use.

The **Polaroid Corp.** of Cambridge, Mass., is manufacturing a $90 folding camera weighing 4 pounds that turns out a finished small photo within one minute.

Transparent cigarette lighters made of lucite are developed.

A space-saving plastic hanger for women's clothing holds a skirt, slip, pair of slacks, two belts and one jacket.

A HONEY FOR EVERY SWEETIE

E.C. Close, a beekeeper from Corning, California, applies for a patent on a process to produce honey in six different colors and flavors, namely strawberry, maple, chocolate, lemon, pineapple and mint.

MAKE MINE GREEN

Chlorophyll gum, candy and toothpaste are popular nationwide.

COFFEE, TEA OR SHAMPOO

Brooklyn company Coffette Products announces the development of coffee-based consumer products ranging from shampoo to laundry detergent using sub-standard coffee that would otherwise be discarded.

★ ★ ★ ★ ★

Popular Ovaltine gets a new competitor by the name of Nestle's Quik chocolate powder to be used in milk.

★ ★ ★ ★ ★

Pepsi Cola sold in cans for the first time.

★ ★ ★ ★ ★

The Bowman Dairy Company of Chicago introduces whipped cream in a throw-away metal container.

★ ★ ★ ★ ★

The McDonald Brothers open hamburger stand in San Bernardino, California serving pre-cooked food instead of preparing food to order. Their menu includes a 15-cent hamburger, 10-cent soft drinks, 20-cent milk shakes and 5-cent coffee.

WHAT A YEAR IT WAS!

FENDER BENDER MENDER

A machine for straightening dented fenders without detaching them from the car is patented by John M. Johnson and Bernard P. Leaf of Lindsborg, Kansas.

MOBILITY FOR POLIO PATIENTS

Poliomyelitis victim Dr. Arthur C. Guyton, University of Mississippi faculty member, designs motorized wheelchair operated by no more than a wiggle of the finger.

★ ★

"Little Lulu" becomes mascot for Kimberly-Clark's Kleenex Tissues.

★ ★

The Dorby Company of Chicago introduces new infra-red electric cooker designed to eliminate cooking odors and cook food 30% to 60% faster.

★ ★

Dial, the first deodorant soap, is introduced to the consumer market.

★ ★ ★ ★ ★ ★ ★ ★ ★ ★ ★ ★ ★ ★ ★ ★ ★

The Air Flow Brush Company announces new paintbrush that eliminates dipping and dripping.

★ ★ ★ ★ ★ ★ ★ ★ ★ ★ ★ ★ ★ ★

A new oil-checking device is developed by the Parkwood Manufacturing Company of Philadelphia which lights up in amber when the oil drops below normal.

★ ★

A cow that moos and gives milk is the latest soft stuffed animal unveiled at the American Toy Fair in New York. Not to be outdone, a New York manufacturer introduces a doll which burps when you pat it on the back.

★ ★

Deaf children at Chicago's Ephpheta School For The Deaf hear a human laugh for the first time through the use of headsets and powerful amplification of a phonograph record.

★ ★

Nikon camera introduced to compete with Leica.

★ ★

Patents are granted for the "Adventure Bra," Vacuum Leaf Raker, Metallic Shoes, Suction Ear Muffs and Fountain Safety Razor.

British optometrist Norman Bier designs contact lenses he claims triples the current five-hour wearing time.

Bausch & Lomb Optical Company announce the development of shaded sunglasses which permit the wearer to look at the sun without discomfort.

RCA develops a stylus (reading pencil) for the blind which shines a slender beam of light on printed letters and then electronically translates the reflected patterns into sounds.

A new type of transformer is developed for fluorescent lamps making instant lighting possible without the preliminary flicker.

Alvin M. Marks of Polarized Illumination of Whitestone, New York, invents a new polarizing material for use in non-glare lighting.

CANCER ANYONE?

Westinghouse announces the development of a new fluorescent sunlamp for use in a special "beauty cabinet" which after two minutes exposure simulates a suntan.

A metal lamp which clamps onto books makes reading in bed possible without disturbing your bedmate.

OW!

George Coffey of Providence, RI, invents a talking typewriter—when you strike a key, it repeats the letters.

Salton Hottray, Solar-Heated Houses and Scrabble make first appearance.

Lockheed announces the development of the double-decker "Constitution"—world's second biggest land-based transport train.

Manhattan's U.S. Hoffman Machine Corp. unveils new dry-cleaning machine predicting it will revolutionize the business by reducing the number of operations involved in cleaning clothes from three to one by consolidating the procedures.

40TH NATIONAL BUSINESS SHOW UNVEILS NEW OFFICE PRODUCTS

1. IBM's Electronic Calculating Punch electronically does multiplication, cross-addition, cross-subtraction and division for the first time.

2. Dictaphone introduces new portable plug-in model capable of recording 15 minutes of dictation on envelope-sized lightweight plastic belts.

3. Soundscriber Dictating Machine with a recording disk capable of being reused many times.

4. Thomas Mechanical Collator introduces machine whose metal fingers can sequence, sort and staple from as many as five piles.

5. IBM's Master Clock which keeps all clocks in a building on time by use of an electronic impulse which it sends out every hour.

New in Cars:

- Porsche Sports Model 356
- Under Dash Air Conditioners
- Land Rover
- Michelin Radial Tires
- Nonglare Headlights
- Heat-Conducting Windshields

The Chesapeake & Ohio Railroad introduces its new family coach cars equipped with movie theaters seating ten children, playroom, diapering room, and tavern-lounge cars with luncheon counters and soda fountains. They also open central reservation office in Huntington, West Virginia allowing passengers to reserve train space by direct out-of-town telephone calls at five cents and to charge fares to their accounts or to pay them after boarding train.

WHAT A YEAR IT WAS!

ARCHITECTURE

Colorful ceramic tiles are popular in bathrooms and kitchens.

Modern furniture has clean, sleek lines, mobility and is often lighter colored than in the past.

The Rhode Island School of Design's Museum of Art has a contemporary furniture exhibit which shows what modern items a typical American couple might purchase. Museum visitors can sit on the furniture and open drawers. The Museum does not claim all pieces are nice.

Birch and plywood are favored woods with modern furniture designers. Other materials include nylon, cotton cord, foam rubber and coil springs.

New York's House of Italian Handicrafts holds a "Summer Living" display showcasing Italian artists from Milan and Turin.

Almost 1 million housing units are built in the U.S.

Prefabricated houses maintain their popularity, allowing for affordable housing at the unfortunate expense of originality.

Harvard's Walter Gropius designs living quarters for graduate students.

Sculptor Isamu Noguchi designs the ceiling in St. Louis' American Stove Company's lobby.

Carl Koch develops the Acorn House, which is folded and transported to its site on a truck.

The "Skipfloor Corridor" plan is used as construction begins on a new building in Cambridge, Mass. Elevators stop on every third floor, allowing more living space in each apartment.

1948

Pasadena, California's new Bullocks Department Store is an example of modern baroque architecture.

An Alexander Calder mobile is incorporated into the design of the Cloud Room Restaurant at Chicago's airport.

Columbia University in New York begins construction on a $1 million building to house students in the various arts.

Sturdy wallpaper is made of steel coated with porcelain enamel. Wallpaper fabrics include velvet, wool, cotton, rayon, chintz and taffeta patterned in plaids, stripes, polka dots, wedgewood, fruit and flowers.

Le Corbusier begins work on a housing unit in Marseilles, France that will be its own community when finished.

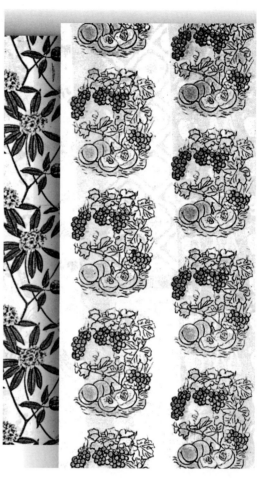

Imaginative kitchens are organized for easy access to utensils and food, with storage and work areas throughout the room. A combination kitchen-laundry room package can be purchased for under $3,000.

France's Salon des Artistes Decorateurs displays the newest in European interior design. Ornate iron work, beautiful woods and exquisite designs are used in classic, intricate and imaginative ways.

ENTERTAINMENT

Cary Grant

Betty Grable

Bob Hope

Abbott & Costello

Spencer Tracy

Top Box Office Stars

Bing Crosby
Betty Grable
Bud Abbott &
Lou Costello
Gary Cooper
Bob Hope
Humphrey Bogart
Clark Gable
Cary Grant
Spencer Tracy
Ingrid Bergman

Stars Of Tomorrow

Ann Blyth
Cyd Charisse
Doris Day
Mona Freeman
Celeste Holm
Angela Lansbury
Eleanor Parker
Jean Peters
Jane Powell
Robert Ryan

In her first film role **Doris Day** sings *"It's Magic"* which hits the charts.

Chuck Jones and **Mike Maltese** introduce their new cartoon characters— **Road Runner** and the **Coyote**.

Johnny Weissmuller turns 44 and makes his 12th and final **Tarzan** film.

Lee Strasberg takes over the Actors Studio and passes on his "Method" technique to some of his young students including **Marlon Brando**, **Paul Newman**, **Joanne Woodward** and **James Dean**.

Paul Newman

Marlon Brando

Rope
Sleep, My Love
Sorry, Wrong Number
Oliver Twist
Sitting Pretty
State Of The Union
T-Men
The Miracle Of The Bells
The Naked City
The Paleface
The Red Shoes
The Search
The Snake Pit
The Three Godfathers
The Time Of Your Life
The Treasure Of The Sierra Madre
THE YOUNG GUARD
Unfaithfully Yours
You Were Meant For Me

105

The Windsor Imperial combines the finest Radio-Phonograph Magnavox ever built with Magnascope—
the new excellence in television. Radio-Phonograph, $895. Bookcase Television Receiver, $750.

The Windsor Imperial Radio-Phonograph.

Perfection in home entertainment

**FOUR HOURS of continuous music from
one loading of new LP records . . . plus
MAGNASCOPE TELEVISION which may
be added to your Magnavox at any time**

MAGNAVOX brings you a great new instrument for home entertainment. This is the first radio-phonograph to play both the new LP (long-playing) and standard 78 rpm records *automatically*. Further, Magnascope television which brings sharper, clearer pictures without glare or eyestrain may be had now or added later.

Only the magnificent Magnavox radio-phonograph and television receivers offer you a wide choice of traditional and modern cabinets, each expertly built to be "at home" with your finest furniture. As you would expect there is no truer, more flawless reception of AM-FM and world-wide Short Wave broadcasts than that given by Magnavox.

Record-playing's greatest innovation in twenty years is yours with Magnavox. You enjoy greater convenience and lower-cost music than ever before! One loading of LP records on the new Duomatic Changer delivers a full evening of *continuous* music. In all models from $375 to $895; other furniture models from $179.50. Television receivers from $299.50 to $750. Write for brochure. The Magnavox Company, Dept. 220, 2133 Bueter Road, Fort Wayne 4, Indiana. *Prices subject to change without notice.*

the magnificent
Magnavox
radio-phonograph + television

The Modular Television Receiver correlated with
Magnavox Cosmopolitan AM-FM Radio-Phonograph.

The Academy Awards For 1948

(For 1947 Films)

BEST PICTURE
Gentleman's Agreement

BEST ACTOR
RONALD COLMAN, *A Double Life*

BEST ACTRESS
LORETTA YOUNG, *The Farmer's Daughter*

BEST DIRECTOR
ELIA KAZAN, *Gentleman's Agreement*

BEST SUPPORTING ACTOR
EDMUND GWENN, *Miracle On 34th Street*

BEST SUPPORTING ACTRESS
CELESTE HOLM, *Gentleman's Agreement*

BEST SONG
"ZIP-A-DEE-DOO-DAH," *Song Of The South*

1948 Favorites (Oscars Presented In 1949)

BEST PICTURE
Hamlet

BEST ACTOR
LAURENCE OLIVIER, *Hamlet*

BEST ACTRESS
JANE WYMAN, *Johnny Belinda*

BEST DIRECTOR
JOHN HUSTON,
The Treasure Of The Sierra Madre

BEST SUPPORTING ACTOR
WALTER HUSTON,
The Treasure Of The Sierra Madre

BEST SUPPORTING ACTRESS
CLAIRE TREVOR, *Key Largo*

BEST SONG
"BUTTONS AND BOWS," *The Paleface*

Laurence Olivier

"And The Winner Is..."

WHAT A YEAR IT WAS!

1948

SPECIAL ACADEMY AWARD HONORS

Sid Grauman, Master Showman, Honored For Raising The Standard Of Exhibition Of Motion Pictures.

Adolph Zukor, The Father Of The Feature Film In America, Is Honored For His Services To The Motion Picture Industry For Over 40 Years.

Marty Martin, Jack Lannan, Russell Shearman And The RKO Radio Studio Special Effects Department Is Honored For The Development Of A New Method Of Simulating Falling Snow.

Nick Kalten, Louis J. Witti And The 20th Century Fox Studio Mechanical Effects Department Are Honored For Developing A Process Of Preserving And Flame-Proofing Foliage.

Women's Press Club Votes **Errol Flynn** and **Rita Hayworth** "The Least Cooperative Actor And Actress Of The Year" While **Dorothy Lamour** and **Glenn Ford** Are Acknowledged As "Most Cooperative."

Errol Flynn

The National Board Of Review Calls Director **Roberto Rossellini's** film *Paisan* The Best Film Artistically Of The Year.

RITA HAYWORTH SUSPENDED BY COLUMBIA FOR FAILING TO REPORT TO LONA HANSON SET.

The Television Research Institute Predicts That Movie Theatres Will Be Almost Empty By 1955.

"**M**ovie Stars Art Exhibit" Kicks Off Opening Of The Beverly Hills Hall Of Art Including Works By **Jane Wyman, Ginger Rogers, Fred MacMurray, Ella Raines, Elizabeth Taylor, Bea Lillie, Hoagy Carmichael, Lionel Barrymore** and **Margaret O'Brian.**

Howard Hughes Closes Biggest Cash Deal In Hollywood History And Buys Control Of RKO For $8,825,690.

Elizabeth Taylor

Drive-In Movies Gain Popularity Across The Nation.

Britain Cancels Movie Tax On Hollywood Films

Harold Wilson, president of England's Board of Trade *(left)*, looks on as Eric Johnston, president of the Motion Picture Association of America, signs a reciprocal agreement which removes the prohibitive 75% British tax on Hollywood films.

Both countries agree that the 4-year pact will be mutually profitable under the terms that return American movies to British audiences.

Eric Johnston voices the satisfaction of both parties to the removal of this barrier to trade: *"The war of films has been settled by mutual cooperation, good will and understanding, just as all wars can be prevented on the same basis. This is not a Wilson victory or a Johnston victory. It is a victory for the American people and the British people."*

WHAT A YEAR IT WAS!

1948

FAMOUS BIRTHS

New York Film Critics' Awards

BEST ENGLISH SPEAKING PICTURE
The Treasure Of The Sierra Madre

BEST ACTRESS
Olivia De Havilland, The Snake Pit

BEST FOREIGN FILM
Paisan (A Roberto Rossellini Film)

Kathy Bates
Bonnie Bedelia
Susan Blakely
Lindsay Crouse
Gerard Depardieu
Barbara Hershey
Mary Beth Hurt
Jeremy Irons
Samuel L. Jackson

Margot Kidder
Sam Neill
Bernadette Peters
John Ritter
Mercedes Ruehl
Dianne Wiest
JoBeth Williams
John Woo

Look,
Up In The Sky—It's A Bird
It's A Plane—
No, It's *Superman!*
And So Begins Columbia's
Newest Serial, SUPERMAN.

Top Ten Films

1 Hamlet
2 The Search
3 Sitting Pretty
4 Gentleman's Agreement
5 Johnny Belinda
6 Joan Of Arc
7 I Remember Mama
8 The Bishop's Wife
9 The Red Shoes
10 The Snake Pit

Passings

D.W. Griffith, pioneer filmmaker and inventor of now standard cinematic techniques such as fade-ins, fade-outs, flashbacks, soft-focus and moving-camera shots dies at age 68. Griffith headed his own Biograph Studios, helped found United Artists and created the masterpiece, "THE BIRTH OF A NATION."

Russian director and visionary **Sergei Eisenstein**, who changed the way films were made with his inventive camera angles and montages, created his masterpiece BATTLESHIP POTEMKIN at age 26 and watched the Soviets ban part of his final film, IVAN THE TERRIBLE, dies at age 49.

Louis Lumiere, widely regarded as having invented motion pictures along with his brother Auguste, dies in France at age 84.

Actor, director and co-founder of the Academy Of Motion Picture Arts And Sciences, **Fred Niblo**, director of BEN HUR and THE THREE MUSKETEERS, dies at age 74.

Actress, European theatre entertainer during World War II and author **Carole Landis** commits suicide at the age of 28 in Brentwood, California.

Edgar Kennedy, U.S. actor and comedian, dies at age 58.

WHAT A YEAR IT WAS!

Ella Fitzgerald

MUSIC

1948 POPULAR SONGS

Ah, But It Happens .... Frankie Laine
Am I Asking Too Much? .... Dinah Washington
Because .... Perry Como
Black Coffee .... Sarah Vaughan
Blue Christmas .... Ernest Tubb
Bouquet Of Roses .... Eddy Arnold
Buttons And Bows .... Dinah Shore
Confess .... Patti Page
The Deck Of Cards .... Tex Ritter
Early Autumn .... Stan Getz
Faraway Places .... Bing Crosby
                                                                  & The Ken Darby Choir
The Fat Man .... Fats Domino
Gloria .... The Mills Brothers
Honky Tonkin' .... Hank Williams
The Huckle Buck .... Frank Sinatra
It's Magic .... Doris Day
It's Too Soon To Know .... Dinah Washington
Lazy River .... Mills Brothers
Mañana .... Peggy Lee
Mansion On The Hill .... Hank Williams
My Happiness .... Ella Fitzgerald
My Darling, My Darling .... Jo Stafford
Nature Boy .... Nat "King" Cole
Now Is The Hour .... Bing Crosby
Oklahoma Waltz .... Patti Page
Once In Love With Amy .... Ray Bolger
The Pretty Mama Blues .... Ivory Joe Hunter
Smoke, Smoke, Smoke
That Cigarette .... Tex Williams
The Streets Of Laredo .... Dennis Day
Twelfth Street Rag .... Pee Wee Hunt

Nat "King" Cole

Frank Sinatra

Dinah Washington

JUST TO MAKE SURE...

You can't blame Dad for wanting to make sure of his evening Milky Way, for he knows what a thrilling treat a Milky Way can be. From the very first bite, you enjoy that rare taste blend of the thick, milk chocolate coating . . . the golden layer of smooth, creamy caramel . . . and the soft, chocolate nougat center, richly flavored with real malted milk. All together, a truly thrilling treat, right down to the last, delightful flavor that lingers in your mouth.

When you crave good candy, eat a

Milky Way

Perry Como

TOP RECORDS

AL JOLSON VOL. III
Al Jolson

MERRY CHRISTMAS
Bing Crosby

A SENTIMENTAL DATE
Perry Como

DOWN MEMORY LANE
Vaughn Monroe

A PRESENTATION OF PROGRESSIVE JAZZ
Stan Kenton

BUSY FINGERS
Three Sons

New Recording Artists
Doris Day
Patti Page
Kay Starr

◇ **Jerry Wayne's** Recording Of *You Can't Be True Dear* Becomes First Dubbed-In Voice Recording To Hit Top 10.

◇ Columbia Records To Release First Two Records By 10-Year Old **Toni Harper** Who Is Signed For Hollywood Musical.

◇ Columbia Records Unveils The 12-Inch 33-1/3 Vinyl LP Disc Capable Of Recording 45-50 Minutes Of Music.

◇ Radio Corporation Of America Introduces 7 Inch 45 RPM Record With Up To Five Minutes Of Music On Each Side.

More POPULAR SONGS

Always Be True In My Fashion

A-You're Adorable

A Dream Is A Wish Your Heart Makes

Baby It's Cold Outside

Cuanto Le Gusta

So In Love

Here I'll Stay

A Tree In The Meadow

I'm Looking Over A Four Leaf Clover

You Can't Be True Dear

On A Slow Boat To China

Woody Woodpecker

Wunderbar

All I Want For Christmas Is My Two Front Teeth

Red Roses For A Blue Lady

1948

Downbeat's Top Performers

DUKE ELLINGTON	MOST POPULAR BAND
BENNY GOODMAN	SOLOIST (CLARINET)
ERROL GARNER	INSTRUMENTALIST (PIANO)
SHELLY MANNE	INSTRUMENTALIST (DRUMS)
FLIP PHILLIPS	INSTRUMENTALIST (SAXOPHONE)
CHARLIE SHAVERS	INSTRUMENTALIST (TRUMPET)
CHARLIE VENTURA	JAZZ GROUP
SARAH VAUGHAN	FEMALE VOCALIST
BILLY ECKSTINE	MALE VOCALIST

Benny Goodman

ALL THAT JAZZ ABOUT ALL THAT JAZZ

Dizzy Gillespie, One Of The Founders Of A Form Of Jazz Called *BeBop*, Plays New York. BeBop Is Defined As Primarily Having The Rhythm Suggested Instead Of Beat Out And Is Usually Loud And Fairly Unmelodic.

Benny Goodman Performs At New York's Paramount Theatre With His New Band, Including Bop In The Repertoire For The First Time.

Stan Kenton Gives A Concert At The Hollywood Bowl.

New York Sees The Closing Of Many Of Its 52nd Street Jazz Clubs.

Louis "Satchmo" Armstrong
Arrives In Nice For The International Jazz Festival

Earl Hines Joins Louis Armstrong's Group.

Louis Armstrong

I GOT THE BLUES AND THAT SURE IS GOOD

♪ Wearing A Gardenia In Her Hair, **Billie Holiday** Makes Her First Appearance To An Overflow Crowd At Manhattan's Carnegie Hall After Her Release From The Federal Reformatory For Women In Alderson, West Virginia Where She Served Time For Drug Possession.

Billie Holiday

♪ **John Lee Hooker's** "Boogie Chillun" Sells Over One Million Copies.

♪ Dubbed The Greatest Folk Singer Of Them All, **Leadbelly's** "Backwater Blues" And "Irene" Are Released By Capitol Records.

WHAT A YEAR IT WAS!

FAMOUS BIRTHS

John Carpenter

Alice Cooper

Daryl Hall

Kenny Loggins

Olivia Newton-John

Stevie Nicks

Todd Rundgren

Leo Sayer

Donna Summer

Mick Taylor

James Taylor

Steven Tyler

Stevie Winwood

Jackson Browne

Barbara Mandrell

Robert Plant

Passings

Folk song archivist and author **John Lomax**, who traveled throughout the U.S. in search of roots music, dies at age 80.

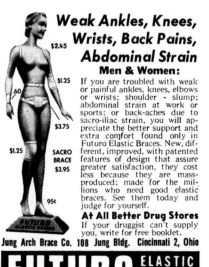

1948

Classical Music

 Due To Severe Budgetary Problems Brilliant Young Conductor **Leonard Bernstein** Resigns As Conductor Of The New York City Symphony And Takes Over As Musical Advisor Of The Israel Symphony Orchestra.

President Of The American Federation Of Musicians, **James Caesar Petrillo**, Signs Three-Year Agreement With Radio Networks Lifting The Ban Against Use Of Musicians In Television.

Negro Conductor **Dean Dixon** Receives The $1,000 Alice M. Ditson Fund Award For The Most Distinguished Service To American Music.

 A Record Number Of Festivals Take Place This Year Including **Sir Ian Hunter's** First BATH INTERNATIONAL MUSIC FESTIVAL.

Music Critics Circle Of New York Vote **Wallingford Riegger's** THIRD SYMPHONY The Most Important New Work Of The 1947-1948 Concert Season.

Walter Piston's SYMPHONY NO. 3 Performed By The Boston Symphony Orchestra Considered The Most Important Of The New American Works.

New Compositions

Sonatas And Interludes
John Cage

Piano Concerto No. 1
Howard Hanson

Three Compositions For Piano
Composition For Twelve Instruments
Milton Babbitt

Sonata For Cello
Elliott Carter

Elegy And Paean For Viola And Orchestra
Roy Harris

Symphony No. 6
William Schuman

Concerto For Clarinet And Strings with harp and piano
Aaron Copland

Louisiana Story
Virgil Thomson

Vier Letzte Lieder
Richard Strauss

Survivor From Warsaw
Arnold Schonberg

String Quartet
Seventh String Quartet
Bohuslav Martinu

Turangalila-Symphony
Olivier Messiaen

MOST POPULAR INSTRUMENTS

Keyboard	73.6%
Wind Instruments	12.0%
Fretted String	11.3%
Bowed String	8.2%
All Others	7.9%

WHAT A YEAR IT WAS!

Admiral triple thrill!

TWO-SPEED PHONOGRAPH...MAGIC MIRROR TELEVISION...FM-AM RADIO

America's Smart Set

ADMIRAL TELEVISION CONSOLES WITH MATCHING RADIO-PHONOGRAPHS

ABOVE—Magic Mirror Television, 10" picture screen. Modern or traditional console. Walnut, $29995

LEFT—New two-speed automatic radio-phonographs in matching consoles as low as $16995

3-Way Portable
Plays instantly on AC or DC, as well as batteries. Beautiful emperor red and French gold case, $3495

FM-AM Radio and Automatic Phonograph
Costs little more than an FM-AM radio alone! Plays up to 12 records automatically with Miracle tone arm. Mahogany $9995

Prices slightly higher in far south

Complete Home Entertainment all in One Luxurious Console $49995 walnut

Installation and one year's service contract extra. Federal tax $5.25.

From Admiral comes *complete* home entertainment to charm your family and guests. Magic Mirror Television brings you bright, steady, mirror-like pictures on a big 10" direct view screen . . . the clearest pictures of them all!

Super-powered by 29 tubes to assure dependable performance even in outlying areas. Receives on *all* channels. New two-speed automatic phonograph plays standard as well as new LP (long play) 45 minute microgroove records. Here, too, is a powerful radio with the finest features in FM-AM as developed by Admiral.

Truly a triple thrill . . . all combined in a breathtakingly beautiful cabinet that measures only 48 inches wide! See it! Hear it! Today!

117

 ## Classical Music Televised For The First Time

Five Years After Sergei Rachmaninoff's Death, EUGENE ORMANDY Conducts The Philadelphia Orchestra In The *D Minor Symphony* For CBS-TV In The First U.S. Symphony Program Ever Televised. WNBT Follows With ARTURO TOSCANINI Conducting The NBC Symphony In An Evening Of Wagner.

Opening Night Of New York City's Metropolitan Opera Production Of Verdi's *Otello* Is Broadcast Live For The First Time.

AND THE CHILDREN SHALL LEAD THEM

9-Year Old FERRUCCIO BURCO, Grandson Of VINCENZO BELLINI, Makes His Carnegie Hall Debut Conducting Wagner And Beethoven.

16-Year Old Hungarian Pianist ERVIN LASZLO Makes Astonishing Debut.

 **RCA Offers New Recording Technique In Tchaikovsky's *Sleeping Beauty* Conducted By LEOPOLD STOKOWSKI.**

 ## Premieres

Knoxville: Summer Of 1915
Samuel Barber, James Agee

Symphony No. 4
David Diamond

Mandu-Carara
Heitor Villa-Lobos

Fantasy For Trombone And Orchestra
Paul Creston

The Seine At Night
Virgil Thomson

Symphony No. 4
George Antheil

Three Symphonic Dances
Norman Dello Joio

Symphony For Classical Orchestra
Harold Shapero

MUSICAL NOTES

National survey of public interest in music reveals the following:

- 30% of nation's families have one or more family members who play an instrument with the percentage rising to 45% for families with annual incomes of over $5,000.

- More women play instruments than men.

- The piano is the most popular instrument.

- Church music is favorite kind of music with popular dance music running a very close second.

- Classical music finishes sixth after Folk, Semiclassical, Operetta, Cowboy and Hillbilly.

Passings

Franz Lehar, whose opera *The Merry Widow* catapulted him to worldwide renown, dies at age 78 in Austria.

Umberto Giordano, Italian composer of the famed opera *Andrea Chenier*, dies in Milan at age 81.

1948

FAMOUS BIRTH

Mikhail Baryshnikov

- ❧ VALERIE BETTIS Considered The Finest Female Dancer On Concert Stage.

- ❧ The Ballet Society Of New York Premieres Igor Stravinsky's New Ballet ORPHEUS Choreographed By GEORGE BALANCHINE.

- ❧ MARTHA GRAHAM Completes Successful Two-Week New York Tour With "Night Journey" Danced To William Schuman's Score.

- ❧ JOSE LIMON Presents "Day On Earth" By Doris Humphrey Danced To A Sonata By Aaron Copland.

- ❧ Ballet Russe de Monte Carlo Celebrates Its Tenth Anniversary.

Dance

Dance Premieres

Concerto Barocco
Choreographer: George Balanchine

Triumph Of Bacchus And Ariadne
Choreographer: George Balanchine
Music: Vittorio Rieti

Symphony In C
Choreographer: George Balanchine
Music: Georges Bizet

Capricorn Concerto
Choreographer: Todd Bolender
Music: Samuel Barber

Orpheus
Choreographer: George Balanchine
Music: Igor Stravinsky

Fall River Legend
Choreographer: Agnes de Mille
Music: Morton Gould

Strangler
Choreographer: Eric Hawkins
Music: Bohuslav Martinu

Wilderness Stair
Choreographer: Martha Graham
Music: Norman Dello Joio

The Ballet Society Finds Permanent Home At New York City Center And Changes Name To New York City Ballet. Members Of The Company Include Maria Tallchief, Tanaquil Le Clercq, Nicholas Magallanes, Francisco Moncion, Herbert Bliss And Todd Bolender. Balanchine's "Serenade," "Orpheus," And "Symphony In C" Kick Off The Season.

Brilliant Choreographer And Innovator In The Use Of Electronic Sound, Alwin Nikolais, Takes Over As Head Of New York's Henry Street Playhouse.

OPERA NEWS

Benjamin Britten's PETER GRIMES Is The Met's First New Opera Of The Year. He Is Proclaimed *"A Wonder Boy Who Will Restore The Glitter To Opera's Tarnished Tiara."*

Gian Carlo Menotti's THE OLD MAID AND THE THIEF Premieres At New York City Opera.

Winners Of The Metropolitan Auditions Of The Air Awards— SOPRANO **Marilyn Cotlow** BARITONE **Frank Guarrera.**

Ezio Pinza Stars In The San Francisco Opera Production Of BORIS GODUNOV And **Tito Gobbi** Makes His Debut In IL BARBIERE DE SIVIGLIA.

Peter Grimes Receives Accolades In London For His New Adaptation Of THE BEGGARS OPERA.

Columbia Records Releases Full-Scale Metropolitan Opera Recording Of LA BOHEME.

Regina Resnik Appears In DIE FLEDERMAUS In Central City, Colorado.

Handsome 26-Year Old Italian Tenor, **Giuseppe Di Stefano** Makes His New York Debut As The Duke In Verdi's RIGOLETTO For Manhattan's Ballet Society.

Igor Stravinsky's MASS Receives Cold Reception At Milan's La Scala.

Milton Berle Hosts The First TEXACO STAR THEATRE Show Scoring A Whopping 86.7 Percent Rating And Takes Over As Permanent Host After A Series Of Rotating Emcees.

Ed Sullivan's TOAST OF THE TOWN Premieres On CBS Introducing Two Unknown Comics—**Dean Martin** And **Jerry Lewis**.

Pianist **Bob Howard** Is First Negro Artist To Host A Network TV Series.

Allen Funt's Successful Radio Show CANDID CAMERA Makes Television Debut.

Perry Como's 15-Minute CHESTERFIELD SUPPER CLUB Makes Television Premiere.

Television Begins Kinescope Recordings Of Programs For Later Pacific Standard Time Broadcast.

The Ajax Commercial Becomes First Popular TV Jingle.

U.S. Weather Bureau Launches First Weather Man–James Fidler– On DuMont Network At 6:05 P.M. Monday Through Friday.

WHATS NEW ON T.V.

Arthur Godfrey's Talent Scouts

Break The Bank

Kukla, Fran & Ollie

Lucky Pup

The Milton Berle Show

The Morey Amsterdam Show

The Original Amateur Hour
(Ted Mack)

Philco Television Playhouse

Studio One

Camel Newsreel Theatre
(John Cameron Swayze)

Douglas Edwards And The News

The Bigelow Show

Wrestling

FAMOUS BIRTHS

Kate Jackson

Susan Lucci

Jerry Mathers

Rhea Perlman

Phylicia Rashad

Sally Struthers

George Wendt

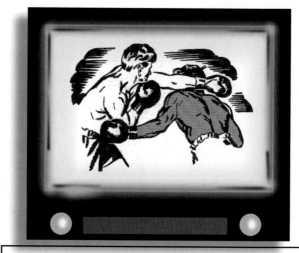

ABC Televises First NFL Football Game.

New York's Paramount Theatre Holds First Televised Public Showing Of A Boxing Match

NBC Launches The New Year With Full-Page Newspaper Ads Proclaiming Network Television As The *"Greatest Medium Of Mass Communication In The World."*

1948

Amos 'N' Andy Sell Their Program To CBS For $2,000,000.

After A 16-Year Association, **Walter Winchell** And The Jergens Co. Agree To Part Ways Because Of Winchell's Refusal To Do A Commercial He Found Offensive For Dryad Deodorant.

Reporters Witness First Use Of A TV Set On A Train.

Pilot Radio Introduces First TV Set To Sell For Under $100 With A Screen Size Of 2" By 3".

RADIO

POPULAR RADIO PROGRAMS

FRED ALLEN
GEORGE BURNS & GRACIE ALLEN
JACK BENNY
BING CROSBY
DUFFY'S TAVERN
FIBBER McGEE & MOLLY
ARTHUR GODFREY
PHIL HARRIS & ALICE FAYE
DOROTHY LAMOUR
LUX RADIO THEATRE

Jack Benny

Lucille Ball

Dorothy Lamour

WHAT A YEAR IT WAS!

1948

- DANNY THOMAS Makes Radio Debut.

- JACK BENNY Sells His NBC Radio Program To CBS For A Reported $2 To $3 Million.

- Broadway's Top Negro Actor Canada Lee Takes Disc Jockey Job On New York's WNEW.

- ERIC SEVAREID Quits As CBS's Washington Bureau Chief To Do Newscasting Full Time.

- FRANK SINATRA Files For License To Operate A One-Kilowatt Daytime Radio Station In Palm Springs.

- NBC And CBS Begin Recording Their Radio Programs For Later Broadcast In Pacific Standard Time.

Radio Premieres

LIFE WITH LUIGI
J. Carrol Naish

THIS IS YOUR LIFE
Ralph Edwards

OUR MISS BROOKS
Eve Arden & Jeff Chandler

MY FAVORITE HUSBAND
Lucille Ball & Gale Gordon

In Radio Tryouts, **Gordon MacRae** Wins Star Billing On The Texaco Show Over **Tony Martin**.

94.2% Of American Families Boast At Least One Radio.

Radio Sets In Use:
75,000,000
TV Sets In Use:
1,000,000

STOP THE MUSIC Premieres On ABC Radio With Host **Bert Parks** Randomly Dialing Listeners Until A Song Is Identified.

WHAT A YEAR IT WAS!

Picasso

AT A FAIR IN THE SOUTH OF FRANCE **PABLO PICASSO** DISPLAYS 39 PIECES OF POTTERY.

THE CITY ART MUSEUM OF ST. LOUIS EXHIBITS OVER 100 OILS, DRAWINGS AND PRINTS BY GERMAN EXPRESSIONIST PAINTER **MAX BECKMANN.**

AUTHOR HENRY MILLER'S WATER-COLORS, INCLUDING PORTRAITS OF ANAIS NIN AND MAN RAY, PAINTED IN BIG SUR, CALIFORNIA, CAN BE VIEWED AT THE 750 STUDIO IN CHICAGO.

LOS ANGELES WELCOMES ITS FIRST CONTEMPORARY ART MUSEUM, THE MODERN INSTITUTE OF ART.

IN BOSTON, THE INSTITUTE OF MODERN ART CHANGES ITS NAME TO THE INSTITUTE OF CONTEMPORARY ART.

THE CLEVELAND MUSEUM OF ART'S BIGGEST SHOW EVER HAS 1293 OBJECTS BY 437 ARTISTS IN WATERCOLOR, SCULPTURE, DECORATIVE ARTS & PHOTOGRAPHY.

THE NEW YORK PUBLIC LIBRARY celebrates its first 100 years with an exhibit of rare pieces. On view are a Gutenberg Bible, a letter written by Christopher Columbus, the Bay Psalm Book and a copy of the Declaration of Independence in Thomas Jefferson's handwriting.

THE LONG AWAITED MERGER between New York's Metropolitan Museum Of Art and the Whitney Museum is called off due to differing philosophies.

BALTIMORE, MARYLAND is home to Laura Gardin Fraser's monument dedicated to Robert E. Lee and "Stonewall" Jackson.

ARCHITECT EERO SAARINEN is the winner of $40,000 in a St. Louis competition, for his *Gateway To The West* design. The memorial will commemorate the Louisiana Purchase, Thomas Jefferson and the opening of the West.

J. Gutenberg

60 PIECES OF SCULPTURE by Gwen Lux, Harold Ambellan, Mark Friedman, Margaret Bassler Kane, William Zorach and others are shown in New York's Washington Square. Admission is 25 cents.

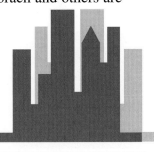

WHAT A YEAR IT WAS!

DAVID DOES DC

Michelangelo's renowned *David* begins its journey to Washington's National Gallery, for a premiere showing at President Truman's January 1949 inauguration. David is escorted to the U.S. on the Navy's USS Grand Canyon.

Mexico City's Hotel del Prado opens, featuring murals by Diego Rivera, while a Joan Miro mural adorns the Terrace Plaza Hotel in Cincinnati.

A collage exhibit is presented by New York's Museum of Modern Art.

ART FOR CHARITY

An exhibit and auction to benefit the Urban League Service Fund features paintings by Joe Louis, Winston Churchill, Dwight Eisenhower, Van Johnson, Clifton Webb, Lena Horne, Bud Shulberg, Noel Coward, George Abbott, Cab Calloway, Joan Crawford, and Claudette Colbert. Eisenhower's work raises $2,600 for the organization.

OY VEY, SUCH A DEAL

Torah covers, spice boxes and a Purim tray sell for $1,800 in New York City.

Jewelry, silverware, porcelain, and glassware stolen from Nazi victims of World War II is sold at auction, with proceeds going to the United Nations' International Refugee Organization.

AMERICA'S LEADING ARTISTS

Stuart Davis	Lyonel Feininger
George Grosz	Yasuo Kuniyoshi
Jack Levine	John Marin
Ben Shahn	Franklin Watkins
Max Weber	

PASSINGS

ABBY GREENE ALDRICH ROCKEFELLER, wife of John D., Jr., philanthropist and co-founder of New York's Museum of Modern Art, dies at age 73.

ARSHILE GORKY, abstract painter, dies by his own hand after a car accident.

Venice Biennale

Venice, Italy is host to the 24th Venice Biennale, the first postwar international exhibition of contemporary art, where works of great artists such as **Henry Moore, Auguste Renoir, Claude Monet, Vincent Van Gogh, Georges Braque, Marc Chagall, Pablo Picasso** and **Paul Klee** can be viewed.

Among the standout American paintings at Venice are:

William Baziotes	Seascapes
Lyonel Feininger	The Church
Arshile Gorky	Argula
George Grosz	Peace No. 2
Edward Hopper	Compartment C, Car 293
Reginald Marsh	Coney Island Beach
Georgia O'Keefe	Sunset
Mark Rothko	Baptismal Scene
Ben Shahn	Reconstruction
Max Weber	Musi
Andrew Wyeth	Spool Bed

Venice Biennale Prize Winners

500,000 Lira Award:

Georges Braque	Magician (painting)
Henry Moore	Family (sculpture)

International Print Prize:
Marc Chagall

126

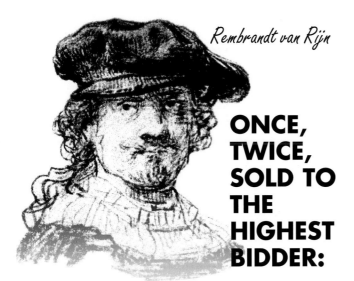

Rembrandt van Rijn

ONCE, TWICE, SOLD TO THE HIGHEST BIDDER:

Jan van der Heyden	*View of Delft*	$15,000
Thomas Gainsborough	*Portrait of a Young Girl*	$13,500
Claude Monet	*Isles on the Seine at Port Villers*	$ 5,080
Edgar Degas	*Mary Cassatt au Louvre*	$ 4,000
French tapestries		$28,500
Rembrandt van Rijn	*Self Portrait*	£13,500
Peter Paul Rubens	*Holy Family*	£ 6,930

ONE-MAN SHOWS OF POPULAR ARTISTS

Alberto Giacometti	*Modern sculpture at its best*
Edward Hopper	*First one-man show in 12 years*
Pablo Picasso	*Premiere of his 1947 paintings*
Henri Matisse	*16 paintings never before seen in America*
Joan Miro	*Old and new abstract paintings*
Willem de Kooning	*New York debut of paintings*
Edouard Manet	*His largest ever show in Manhattan*
Gustave Courbet	*Biggest U.S. show to date*

IMPORTANT ACQUISITIONS

Boston Museum of Fine Arts
TITIAN: *St. Catherine of Alexandria*
Minneapolis Institute of Arts
DEGAS: *Mlle. Valpincon as a Child*
MATISSE: *White Plumes*
Chicago Art Institute
CEZANNE: *portrait of his wife (untitled)*
Cleveland Museum
VAN GOGH: *Road Menders*
Museum of Modern Art
BRAQUE: *Woman with Mandolin*

1948 ADVERTISEMENT

PEOPLE'S CHOICE

Seems as though nearly everybody wants Dodge All-Fluid Drive!

Dodge All-Fluid Drive takes the fight out of stop-and-go traffic driving . . . gives you smoother starts and stops with less gear shifting. Yet this important engineering advance is yours at no extra cost.

Experience Dodge All-Fluid Drive for yourself. Check the many other Dodge extra-value features . . . extra-roomy interiors . . . full-width "Chair-Height" seats . . . welcome head room and leg room . . . oversize luggage compartment.

Discover first hand why owners are so enthusiastic about today's big Dodge!

Dodge

Lowest Priced Car With Fluid Drive
Safe-Guard Hydraulic Brakes, Super-Cushion Tires,
Safety Rim Wheels, Floating Power,
Full-Floating Ride, gyrol Fluid Drive

Notable Paintings

Andrew Wyeth	*Christina's World*
Willem de Kooning	*Woman*
Jackson Pollock	*Composition #1, Nov. 1, 1948*
Edward Hopper	*Seven A.M.*

1948

books

George Orwell
1984

Harold Laski
THE AMERICAN DEMOCRACY

Geoffrey Gorer
THE AMERICAN PEOPLE

H.L. Mencken
THE AMERICAN LANGUAGE
SUPPLEMENT TWO

Jean-Paul Sartre
ANTI-SEMITE AND JEW

Aldous Huxley
APE AND ESSENCE

Lloyd C. Douglas
THE BIG FISHERMAN

Terence Rattigan
THE BROWNING VERSION

W. Somerset Maugham
CATALINA

Robert Penn Warren
THE CIRCUS IN THE ATTIC

Gore Vidal
THE CITY AND THE PILLAR

Frank O'Connor
THE COMMON CHORD, STORIES
AND TALES OF IRELAND

Dwight D. Eisenhower
CRUSADE IN EUROPE

Alan Paton
CRY, THE BELOVED COUNTRY

Nicholas Monsarrat
DEPENDS WHAT YOU
MEAN BY LOVE

Dagobert D. Runes, editor
THE DIARY AND SUNDRY
OBSERVATIONS OF
THOMAS A. EDISON

L.B. Namier
DIPLOMATIC PRELUDE 1938-1939

Thomas Mann
DOCTOR FAUSTUS

Eleanor Green
DORA

George Stewart
FIRE

Margery Sharp
THE FOOLISH GENTLEWOMAN

Winston S. Churchill
THE GATHERING STORM

John Cobb Harper
THE GESTURE

Louis P. Lochner, editor
THE GOEBBELS DIARY

John Dos Passos
THE GRAND DESIGN

Josephine Pinckney
GREAT MISCHIEF

Carl Van Doren
THE GREAT REHEARSAL

James Gould Cozzens
GUARD OF HONOR

Norman Vincent Peale
A GUIDE TO CONFIDENT LIVING

Virgil Carrington Jones
THE HATFIELDS AND THE MCCOYS

Graham Greene
THE HEART OF THE MATTER

Dale Carnegie
HOW TO STOP WORRYING
AND START LIVING

Thornton Wilder
THE IDES OF MARCH

A.L. Baker
INNOCENTS

William Faulkner
INTRUDER IN THE DUST

Irving Brant
JAMES MADISON: THE NATIONALIST

Jean Cocteau
LES PARENTS TERRIBLES

Giovanni Guareschi
THE LITTLE WORLD OF DON CAMILLO

Jean Cocteau

U.S. Consumers Buy
135 Million Paperback
Books This Year.

William Faulkner
Becomes A Member Of
The American Academy
Of Arts And Letters
Along With John
Steinbeck, Mark Van
Doren And Leon Kroll.

Famous Birth

James Ellroy

Charles Austin Beard, best-selling historical author of *THE RISE OF AMERICAN CIVILIZATION* and National Institute of Arts and Letters gold medal winner, dies at age 73 in Connecticut.

Best-selling author **Ross Lockridge**, whose *RAINTREE COUNTY* is one of the most important books of 1948, takes his own life at age 33.

WHAT A YEAR IT WAS!

1948

Evelyn Waugh
THE LOVED ONE

Walter Francis Frear
MARK TWAIN AND HAWAII

Remy
MEMOIRS OF A SECRET AGENT
OF FREE FRANCE

Harold Acton
MEMOIRS OF AN AESTHETE

Antonina Vallentin
MIRABEAU

Martin Buber
MOSES

W.R. Inge
MYSTICISM IN RELIGION

Mark Twain

Norman Mailer
THE NAKED AND THE DEAD

Jawaharlal Nehru
NEHRU ON GANDHI

Arthur Keith
A NEW THEORY OF
HUMAN EVOLUTION

Lancelot Law Whyte
THE NEXT DEVELOPMENT IN MAN

Nevil Shute
NO HIGHWAY

T.S. Eliot
NOTES TOWARD THE
DEFINITION OF CULTURE

Lawrence Durrell
ON SEEMING TO PRESUME

Upton Sinclair
ONE CLEAR CALL

Truman Capote
OTHER VOICES, OTHER ROOMS

Victor Gollancz
OUR THREATENED VALUES

Pearl S. Buck
PEONY

Betty MacDonald
THE PLAGUE AND I

Andre Malraux
PSYCHOLOGIE DE L'ART

Helen Landreth
THE PURSUIT OF ROBERT EMMET

Ross Lockridge, Jr.
RAINTREE COUNTY

Carl Sandburg
REMEMBRANCE ROCK

William Vogt
ROAD TO SURVIVAL

Esther Forbes
THE RUNNING OF THE TIDE

Thomas Merton
SEVEN STOREY MOUNTAIN

Alfred C. Kinsey
SEXUAL BEHAVIOR IN THE
HUMAN MALE

C.S. Forester
THE SKY AND THE FOREST

Joseph George Hitrec
SON OF THE MOON

Merle Miller
THAT WINTER

Howard Spring
THERE IS NO ARMOUR

Dr. Seuss
THIDWICK, THE
BIG-HEARTED MOOSE

Erskine Caldwell
THIS VERY EARTH

Jeannette Mirsky
TO THE ARCTIC!

Betty Smith
TOMORROW WILL BE BETTER

Damon Runyon
TRIALS AND
OTHER TRIBULATIONS

Victoria Case & Robert Case
WE CALLED IT CULTURE

THE WHITE HOUSE PAPERS OF
HARRY L. HOPKINS
(PUBLISHED FOR THE FIRST TIME)

Martha Gelhorn
WINE OF ASTONISHMENT

Irwin Shaw
THE YOUNG LIONS

PRIZES

NOBEL

Literature:

T. S. ELIOT (BRITAIN)
*"FOR HIS OUTSTANDING, PIONEER
CONTRIBUTION TO PRESENT-DAY POETRY."*

PULITZER

Letters:

JAMES A. MICHENER

*Tales Of The
South Pacific*

Poetry:

W. H. AUDEN

The Age Of Anxiety

History:

BERNARD DE VOTO
*Across The Wide
Missouri*

Journalism:

ST LOUIS POST-DISPATCH

Reporting:

GEORGE E. GOODWIN
Atlanta Journal

Editorial Cartooning:

RUBE GOLDBERG
NY Sun

**Saturday Review
of Literature
Book-of-the-Year**

ROBERT E. SHERWOOD
*Roosevelt And
Hopkins*

WHAT A YEAR IT WAS!

129

1948

ON BROADWAY

CHARLES BOYER MAKES
FIRST APPEARANCE ON
AMERICAN STAGE IN
RED GLOVES

FRENCH EXISTENTIALIST,
JEAN~PAUL SARTRE,
DOMINATES THE
AMERICAN STAGE

OKLAHOMA
CELEBRATES FIFTH
YEAR ON BROADWAY

**Charles
Boyer**

ANOTHER OPENING, ANOTHER NIGHT

ANNE OF THE THOUSAND DAYS

Rex Harrison

THE MADWOMAN OF CHAILLOT

Martita Hunt

Patricia Morison and Alfred Drake

KISS ME, KATÉ

Pulitzer Prize for Drama
Tennessee Williams
A STREETCAR NAMED DESIRE

New York Drama Critics' Circle Award
Best Play
Tennessee Williams
A STREETCAR NAMED DESIRE

Best Foreign Play
Terence Rattigan
THE WINSLOW BOY

BROADWAY OPENINGS

Anne Of The Thousand Days
Maxwell Anderson
✵

As The Girls Go
Bobby Clark
✵

Bravo
Edna Ferber & George Kaufmann
✵

The Cup Of Trembling
Louis Paul
✵

Edward, My Son
Robert Morley & Noel Langley
✵

Goodbye, My Fancy
Starring Madeleine Carroll
✵

The Hallams
Rose Franken
✵

Inside U.S.A.
Howard Dietz & Arthur Schwartz
✵

Kiss Me, Kate
Music by Cole Porter
✵

The Leading Lady
Ruth Gordon

WHAT A YEAR IT WAS!

Lend An Ear

☆

Life With Mother
Russel Crouse & Howard Lindsay

☆

Light Up The Sky
Moss Hart

☆

The Linden Tree
J.P. Priestley

☆

Look, Ma, I'm Dancin'

☆

Love Life
Alan Jay Lerner & Kurt Weill

☆

The Madwoman Of Chaillot
Jean Giraudoux

☆

Magdalena
Score by Villa-Lobos

☆

Make Mine Manhattan
Arnold Horwitt & Richard Lewine

☆

Me And Molly
Gertrude Berg

☆

Mister Roberts
From book by Thomas Heggen

☆

My Romance
Sigmund Romberg

1948

Boston Censors Ban Two Lines From Noel Coward's DESIGN FOR LIVING—"Wanton Abode" And An "Unpremeditated Roll In The Hay."

The "Festival Adjuncts" Portion Of The Edinburgh Festival Become Known As The "Fringe."

FAMOUS BIRTH

ANDREW LLOYD WEBBER

1948 TONY AWARDS

OUTSTANDING PLAY
Mister Roberts
Thomas Heggen & Joshua Logan, playwrights

OUTSTANDING PERFORMANCE BY AN ACTOR
Henry Fonda (Mister Roberts)
Paul Kelly (Command Decision)
Basil Rathbone (The Heiress)

OUTSTANDING PERFORMANCE BY AN ACTRESS
Judith Anderson (Medea)
Katharine Cornell (Antony and Cleopatra)
Jessica Tandy (A Streetcar Named Desire)

DISTINGUISHED MUSICAL STAGE PERFORMANCE
Paul Hartman (Angel in the Wings)
Grace Hartman (Angel in the Wings)

OUTSTANDING PERFORMANCE BY NEWCOMERS
June Lockhart (For Love or Money)
James Whitmore (Command Decision)

OUTSTANDING DIRECTOR
Josh Logan (Mister Roberts)

OUTSTANDING DANCE DIRECTION
Jerome Robbins (High Button Shoes)

PASSINGS

1920's Ziegfeld Follies star MARY EATON dies at 46.

British actress DAME MAY WHITTY, star of stage in London and New York as well as Hollywood movies, dies at age 82.

Distinguished Cambridge educated British actor SIR C. AUBREY SMITH, star of stage and screen, business manager and cricket player, dies at age 85.

SUSAN GLASPELL, Pulitzer Prize-winning playwright, active in creating what was to become "Off Broadway" in protest of Broadway commercialism, dies at age 66.

The Old Lady Says "No!"
Denis Johnston (presented by Dublin Gate Theatre)

✬

Power Without Glory
English Production

✬

The Rape Of Lucretia
Book: R. Duncan, Music: B. Britten

✬

Red Gloves
Jean-Paul Sartre

✬

The Respectful Prostitute
Jean-Paul Sartre

✬

Set My People Free
Dorothy Heyward

✬

The Silver Whistle
Robert E. McEnroe

✬

Skipper Next To God
Jan de Hartog

✬

Summer And Smoke
Tennessee Williams

✬

Where's Charley
Starring Ray Bolger

✬

The Young And Fair
N. Richard Nash

1948

DISASTERS

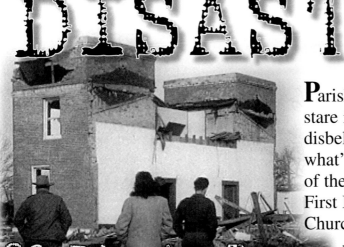

Parishioners stare in disbelief at what's left of their First Baptist Church.

20 Die As Tornadoes Sweep Five Southern States Causing Millions In Property Damage

Hundreds are left homeless in Cotton Valley.

This small American town faces the task of rebuilding itself from the ground up.

New York Bound Dutch KLM Airliner Goes Down In Tarbolton, Scotland Killing 34 Of 40 Passengers.

43 People, Including Theatrical Producer Earl Carroll, Die When A DC-6 Plane Crashes And Burns.

Prince Alfred Hohenlohe zu Schillingsfuerst Of Vienna Among The 39 Passengers And Crew Killed In A Royal Dutch Plane Crash Near Prestwick, Scotland During A Radar-Guided Landing.

Grandson Of President Theodore Roosevelt Among The 35 People Killed In The Crash Of A Chinese Airliner En Route From Shanghai To Hong Kong.

13 Drown As Mississippi Towboat *Natchez* Rolls Over And Sinks In 30 Seconds As Raging River Smashes Vessel Into Bridge.

Steamship *Cautin* Sinks In The Imperial River Near Puerto Saavedra, Chile Drowning An Estimated 150 People.

250 Passengers Of The Japanese Vessel *Joo Maru* Are Missing After The Ship Strikes A Floating Mine And Sinks Near Okayama, Japan.

In Denmark's Worst Shipping Disaster More Than 140 People Are Killed When The Passenger Ship *Kjoebenhavn* Strikes A Mine.

The U.S. Suffers Greatest Loss Of Property Destroyed By Fires In Any One Year.

Explosion In Farben, Germany Chemical Plant Kills 250 And Injures 6,000.

34 People Die As Fire Sweeps Through Home For The Aging In St. John's, Newfoundland.

Trieste, Yugoslavia Coal Mine Site Of Explosion That Kills 71 Miners.

21 Men Die When A Japanese World War II Booby Trap Explodes On Corregidor Island.

Camphor Oil Explodes On Train Near Keelung, Formosa Burning 60 Persons To Death While An Undisclosed Number Drown When They Jump Into A River Over Which The Train is Passing.

Two Boys Confess To Setting A Fire In Reno, Nevada That Kills Five And Injures 180.

A Hong Kong Warehouse Is The Scene Of Fire And Explosion That Kills 135, Injures 57 With Property Damage Estimated At $4,000,000.

At Least 1,100 People Are Missing And Presumed Dead After An Explosion Rips Through Refugee Steamer *Kiagya* En Route From Shanghai In The China Sea.

WHAT A YEAR IT WAS!

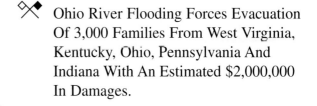

⚔ Smoke And Fog Descend On Donora, Pennsylvania Killing 20 People With 400 Others Needing Medical Treatment.

⚔ 300 People Die And Tens Of Thousands Are Left Homeless On Reunion Island In The Indian Ocean In The Wake Of A Hurricane That Devastates The Island.

⚔ The Cholera Death Toll Rises To 1,374 In One Week In The Province Of Madras, India.

⚔ In Columbia, Oregon More Than 60,000 People Become Homeless When Dikes Give Way In Basin Flood Zone Causing $75 Million In Damage.

⚔ Ohio River Flooding Forces Evacuation Of 3,000 Families From West Virginia, Kentucky, Ohio, Pennsylvania And Indiana With An Estimated $2,000,000 In Damages.

⚔ Up To 100 People Die As A Result Of Eruption Of The Villarrica Volcano And Ensuing Flash Floods.

⚔ 14 Spectators Are Killed And 35 Injured When Racing Cars Skid On Muddy Track In Porto Alegre, Brazil.

⚔ Over 3,000 Lives Are Lost And More Than 10,000 People Are Injured When An Earthquake Destroys Over 19,000 Buildings In Thirty Seconds In The Silk Center Of Fukui, Japan.

⚔ Thousands Are Left Homeless As Floods Sweep Southeastern U.S.

ENGLISH AIRWAYS PLANE CRASHES EN ROUTE FROM GLASGOW

Remains of English Airways plane after crash en route from Glasgow.

The pilot is killed as he brings in plane for belly landing, saving the lives of 17 passengers.

The feminine TOUCH

*D*ad's two best girls have a way with them ... such a way that it's a pleasure to write out their Easter-shopping check! A man likes to see his women folks well-dressed, and when they choose fine-loomed Pacific worsteds and woolens, as he does, the check need not be as large as you would expect.

The Pacific label on a garment is your assurance of smartness, top quality, and generous value in the fabric. Look for it when *you* shop! Pacific Mills, Worsted Division, Dept. K3, 261 Fifth Avenue, New York 16.

Where you will find the Pacific Label

IN WOMEN'S WEAR... Pacific Craft Fabrics in high-style coats and suits. Also more popular priced woolens and worsteds in dresses, skirts, coats, suits and sportswear in women's, misses' and girls' sizes.

IN MEN'S WEAR... excellent quality woolens and worsteds in such clothing brands as Plateau, Surrétwill, Mohara. Also in topcoats, rain coats, slacks, play shorts, swim shorts... new Pacifixed* (wool-washable) fabrics in sport shirts and robes.

*REG. U. S. PAT. OFF.

Pacific Worsteds Woolens

LOOK TO THE fabric FIRST

Fashion

SUITS ME FINE

Narrow Skirt
With Curved
Jacket And
Small Waist

Soft, Full Skirt
With Soft Jacket

Famous Birth: DONNA KARAN

Key Words For A Fashionable '48

Belted & Fitted Coats
•
Bolero Jacket
•
Cape
•
Cardigan Jacket
•
Color
•
Colored Stockings

Crystal Jewelry
•
Cuffed Sleeve
•
Dolman Sleeve
•
Dress-up
•
Femininity
•
Flowers
•
Gauntlet

Lace Handkerchief
•
Lace Patterned Stockings
•
Large Collar
•
Opera Pump
•
Patent Leather

Petite Waistline
•
Pleats
•
Round Shoulders
•
Sash
•
Scarf
•
Shantung
•
Small Handbag

Swan-Neck Shirt
•
Sword Sheath
Umbrella
•
Thin Belt
•
Waistcoat

Dresses

Empire Waist

Lamp-Shade

Coat

Bat-Wing

Princess

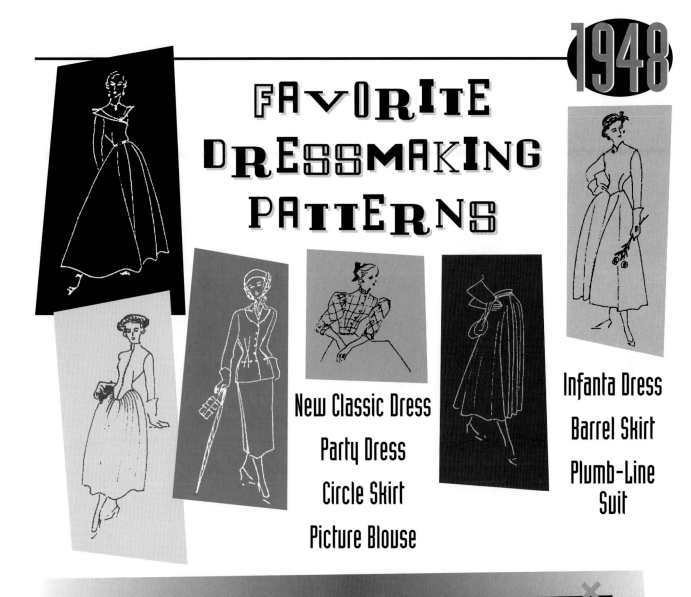

FAVORITE DRESSMAKING PATTERNS

New Classic Dress

Party Dress

Circle Skirt

Picture Blouse

Infanta Dress

Barrel Skirt

Plumb-Line Suit

A MIDSUMMER NIGHT'S TRI-COLORED DREAM

BLACK, WHITE and NATURAL

Are The Three Colors That Will Get You Through The Dog Days Of Summer. Mix And Match The Colors Or Go For The One Color Look—All Black, All White, All Natural. Textures Will Add Variety—With Leather, Straw, Lace, Linen And Beads Leading The Way In Creating A Stylish Ensemble.

Sweater Styles for 1948 Unveiled in Coral Gables, Florida

A cotton pullover with matching cardigan.

A cotton pullover with hood.

A couple of "striking" sweaters

Something for the "horsey" set

142

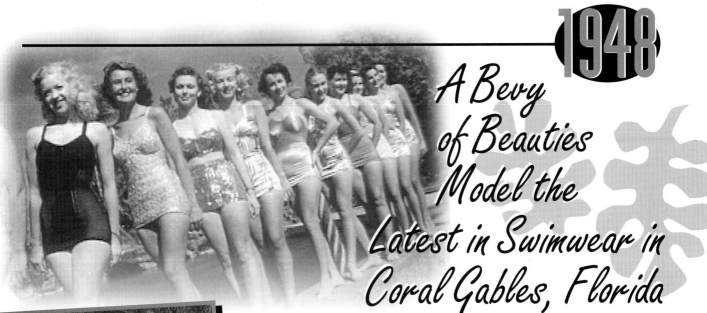

A Bevy of Beauties Model the Latest in Swimwear in Coral Gables, Florida

Eat your heart out, Arthur Godfrey.

This glittering two-piece needs a little pick up.

A lovely mesh one-piece is given full justice by a beautiful blonde.

This is what you can expect to see on your beaches this summer.

The models swing and sway in this tropical paradise.

QUALITY
CRAFTSMANSHIP
STYLE

Forstmann
100% VIRGIN WOOL

Look for this label...it identifies
the finest woolens in the world

FORSTMANN WOOLEN COMPANY
PASSAIC, N.J.

The "Going-Away" Look Turns Many A Man's Head To View The Attractive Styling On The Back Of Skirts.

WHAT DO MEN WANT?

Feminine Figures
Pretty Silhouettes
Decorative & Chic Fashions
Color
A Fashionable,
Yet Original Style
Well-Groomed Appearance

SPRING Sees The Arrival Of Checks For Dresses, Suits And Coats, Worn With Solid-Color Accessories.

HOW ABOUT A PAPER BAG OVER MY HEAD?

If Most Men Agree With Radio's Ted Malone, Women Might Choose To Skip This Fashion Nightmare:

"Who On Earth Are The Droopy Dresses Designed For? A Short Person Looks Like A Gnome; A Tall Person Looks Like A Skyscraper; A Fat Person Looks Like A Tub; A Thin Person Like A Beanpole."

Bi-colored spectator opera

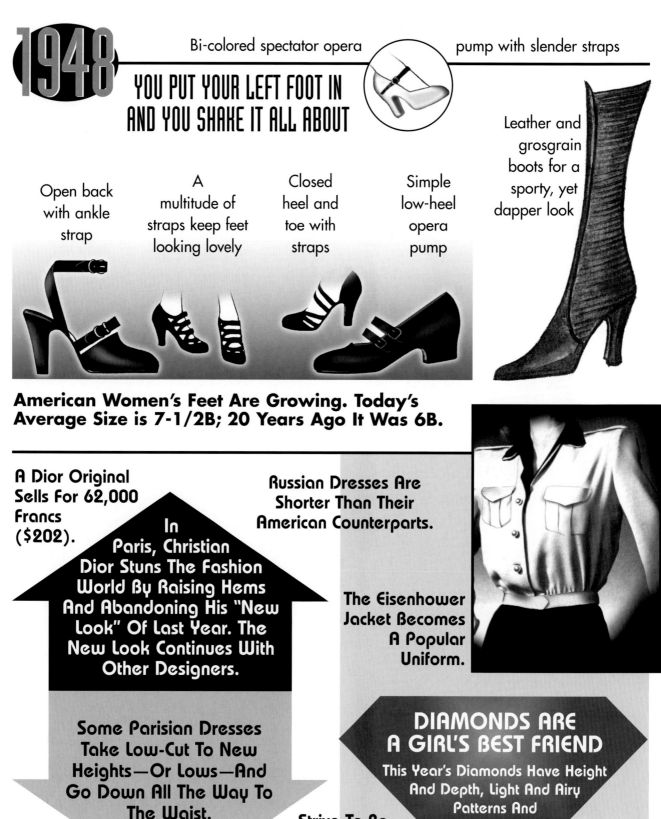

pump with slender straps

YOU PUT YOUR LEFT FOOT IN AND YOU SHAKE IT ALL ABOUT

Open back with ankle strap

A multitude of straps keep feet looking lovely

Closed heel and toe with straps

Simple low-heel opera pump

Leather and grosgrain boots for a sporty, yet dapper look

American Women's Feet Are Growing. Today's Average Size is 7-1/2B; 20 Years Ago It Was 6B.

A Dior Original Sells For 62,000 Francs ($202).

Russian Dresses Are Shorter Than Their American Counterparts.

In Paris, Christian Dior Stuns The Fashion World By Raising Hems And Abandoning His "New Look" Of Last Year. The New Look Continues With Other Designers.

The Eisenhower Jacket Becomes A Popular Uniform.

Some Parisian Dresses Take Low-Cut To New Heights—Or Lows—And Go Down All The Way To The Waist.

DIAMONDS ARE A GIRL'S BEST FRIEND
This Year's Diamonds Have Height And Depth, Light And Airy Patterns And Are Set In Palladium.

French Designer Jacques Fath Displays A Risqué Approach To His Skirts, Slitting The Backs Above The Knee.

Strive To Be A Woman Who People Remark Is "Beautifully Dressed," Not One Who Simply Has "Beautiful Clothes."

Knee-Length Stockings Are Held In Place With An Elastic Band At The Top.

the shoe with the beautiful fit *

The kind of quality and style you like to wear, at the levelheaded prices you don't mind paying. Naturalizer Division, Brown Shoe Company, St. Louis.

Shoes illustrated, 10⁹⁵ to 11⁹⁵
Other styles from 7⁹⁵ to 11⁹⁵

Naturalizer ®

* looks good from any angle

Young lady shoes ... worn with
a delicate air that tells a man
you're lovely. Why not live in
Paradise—the fashion classics
so downright *fitting* for you!

Paradise Shoes

$11⁹⁵ to $16⁹⁵

At finer stores everywhere or write
for name of your nearest dealer.
Brauer Bros. Shoe Co., St. Louis, Mo.

RAT-A-TAT-TAT, OH WHAT A LOVELY HAT

**A Covered
Head Is A
Fashionable
Head. Choices
Include The Bonnet, Cloche,
"Rooftop Of Paris," Sailor, Skimmer,
Veiled, Big And Carriage.**

WHAT A YEAR IT WAS!

HatS On In New Orleans

1948

A *parade kicks off Spring Fashion Week in New Orleans...*

The parade's accent is on the latest spring millinery.

Even the horses get into the hat act.

With the picture hat destined to frame the faces of the American woman this spring and summer, these models assemble in Jackson Square to show off the newest designs by the 19 visiting designers who joined forces to present a preview of Easter finery.

A This charming hat entitled "Chameleon" says it with flowers.

B Gracie Allen models this cute little number to be auctioned off for charity.

C This straw with ribbon trim is also on the charity auction block.

D This chapeau is called "Audubon Handicap."

E For those who prefer the brimless look, there's "Down On The Levee"—salute to "Old Man River."

F This gorgeous straw with organza trim is called "Plantation Party."

G This bonnet with an organza tie fetches a fetching price.

WHAT A YEAR IT WAS!

149

1948

Out Of Sight Fashions

The '48 Figure Is Smaller Than Ever—With The Help Of Undergarments. Your Small Waist, A MUST With Today's Fashions, Is Created With The Help Of Waist-Liners, Girdles, Busks And Figure Capsules.

The Camisole Makes A Comeback, Prettier, Sheerer And More Feminine Than In Grandmother's Day.

Clothing chain **ROBERT HALL CLOTHES, INC.** has 52 stores across the country. The stores are simple, as is the philosophy—lots of clothes at low prices. Robert Hall only carries suits, coats and dresses, with prices ranging from $4.95-13.95 for women's dresses to $22.95-38.95 for men's suits and topcoats.

COTY AMERICAN FASHION CRITICS' AWARD (The "Winnie")
Hattie Carnegie

Film Star **Lauren Bacall** Decides Against Wearing Ugly Maternity Clothes And Designs Her Own Apparel. Lauren's Secret Is To Work With Her Body's New Shape, Instead Of Hiding It.

Summer Fashions For Men

Summer Hats include the Panama and Boater. Boaters are worn with wide, colorful bands.

On The Golf Course he'll wear a linen cap and knickers, with lisle and cotton mesh shirts, or the new open weave fish-net shirt from the south of France.

Sports Shirts are made of rayon, lightweight wool gabardine, broadcloth and silk.

Accessorize with ties, bow-ties and scarves.

Irish Linen slacks in red, white, blue and yellow.

Suits made of seersucker, burma cloth and rayon.

SUGAR AND SPICE AND EVERYTHING NICE

Young Ladies Look Best At Parties With Cotton And Lace Dresses, Sometimes With A Paisley Print. Coats Can Be Flannel, With Large Faux Pearl Buttons.

Arrow's Style of the Month
"Harvest Tones"

WHEN YOU'RE shooting for "Best-dressed Barn Dancer"—or just want to have shirt, tie, and handkerchief teamed up in A-1 taste—get the Arrow "Harvest Tones" ensemble! The shirt pattern is a fresh, new 3-way white satin stripe on broadcloth in blue, gray, tan, green, or wine. Ties and handkerchiefs are teamed up to make a superb combination! Shirts: $4.50.

SHIRTS: each has that *terrific*, that *unparalleled* Arrow Collar, MITOGA — the body tapered fit, and is labeled *Sanforized* (fabric shrinkage less than 1%!).

TIES: three related pattern groups made of soft, luxurious rayon: (1) striped scroll patterns; (2) rich, "embossed" figures; (3) lively chain circles. $1.50.

HANDKERCHIEFS: Arrow "Harvest Tones" handkerchiefs pick up the same smart satin stripe patterns of the shirts. And they're King-size, the way men like 'em. 65¢. *Cluett, Peabody & Co., Inc.*

Look for the Arrow Trade-mark
Arrow—Mitoga—Sanforized: Reg. Trade-marks

ARROW "Harvest Tones" SHIRTS
TIES · HANDKERCHIEFS

Mirror, Mirror On The Wall, Make Me The Fairest One Of All.

Hair Is Worn Short With 1" Bangs That Resemble A Character From An Impressionist Painting.

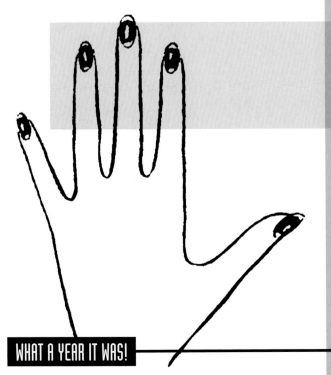

Make-Up Is Entering A Lighter Time, With Lots Of Pink In Lipsticks, Powders And Nail Polishes. Coral Tinged With A Pinkish-Orange Tone Is Also Fashionable. Rouge, A Necessity Now, Should Match Your Lipstick.

Subtle And Tasteful Mascara, Eye Shadows And Eyebrow Pencils Are Guaranteed To Create A Well-Made Up Face.

Body Bronzes And Leg Make-Up Are The Surest Ways To A Quick And Even Tan.

WHAT A YEAR IT WAS!

1948 ADVERTISEMENT

Go Bears!!

*T*oday's College Girl Has Much To Think About, And Doesn't Have Time To Read Fashion Magazines Everyday. By Following These Simple Fashion Rules, She'll Be Ready For A Soda With The Girls Or A Study Session With That Special Someone.

1. The Belted-In Waist
2. Full Skirt, No Longer Than 12" From The Ground
3. Tweed Dresses, Suits Or Coats
4. Shoes With Dainty High Heels
5. Tailored Dresses And Suits For Evenings
6. Berets

WHAT A YEAR IT WAS!

SPORTS

Baseball Loses The Great "Babe" Ruth

100,000 fans file through Yankee Stadium to pay their last respects to *"Bambino,"* baseball's famed George Herman "Babe" Ruth, who dies at 53 after losing his bout with throat cancer. With seven league pennants and four World Series championships, Yankee Stadium became known as "the house that Ruth built."

"Babe" Ruth Career Highlights

1916: Pitches 29 consecutive scoreless innings in World Series for Boston Red Sox. 1.75 ERA. Ruth is made outfielder.

1919: Sets major league record of 29 home runs.

1920: Boston trades the "Sultan of Swat" to Yankees; breaks his own record with 54 home runs.

1926-1931: Breaks all records averaging 50 homers a year.

1927: Leads the league in runs batted in for six seasons; sets all time single season walk record.

1935: Leaves the Yankees and plays briefly with Boston Braves.

1938: Coaches for Brooklyn Dodgers.

1948: 50,000 fans show up at Yankee Stadium to honor the "Babe." The Yankees retire Ruth's No. 3 and send his uniform to the Baseball Hall of Fame in Cooperstown, New York.

WE'D LIKE YOU TO MEET VIRGINIA FELLER, wife of the famous big league pitcher and ex-Navy gunner. Here she is at home in Waukegan, Ill. with their two sons, Stevie, 3, and Marty, 1. We'd like you to meet the Fellers because in many ways they are typical of the 10½ million new families that have appeared on the American scene during the last 8 years. In these inflated times they all have this one great problem — how to get the most for the money they must spend.

To the girl who married Bob Feller

Dear Mrs. Feller:

Have you ever wondered what happens to the money you spend for groceries? As one woman to another, I think you have every right to know.

You, and the millions of others who bought our products last year, helped build General Mills' sales to a record $458,473,576. Where did this money go?

Most of it went to suppliers of raw materials and services needed to make our products. We paid them $389,628,821--85% of our "sales income" --in exchange for their grain, bags, cartons, transportation and so on.

The second largest share of sales income--about 9%, or $42,166,799--was paid in wages and salaries to the 12,000 men and women who "run the business." This figure, by the way,

was 7 times as large as the share that went to our 13,000 stockholders.

Profits, as usual, were under 3¢ on each dollar of sales. Less than half of these earnings went to our stockholders; the rest was reinvested in the business. (For a breakdown of our sales dollar, see chart at right.)

In closing, Mrs. Feller, let me assure you that we here at General Mills are doing everything we can to see that you and all the homemakers of America get full value for every penny you spend for our products.

Sincerely,

Betty Crocker

How the General Mills sales dollar was divided last year

85¢ RAW MATERIALS SUPPLIES & SERVICES

9¢ EMPLOYEES

2.5¢ TAXES

WEAR & TEAR

1.5¢ STOCKHOLDERS

1¢ FUTURE DEVELOPMENT

Baseball

CLEVELAND INDIANS BEAT BOSTON BRAVES 4-2 WINNING THE WORLD SERIES

TAKE ME OUT TO THE BALLGAME
63.8 Million Baseball Fans Flock To Games

Writers' Association Of America Most Valuable Player Award

American League
Lou Boudreau   Cleveland Indians

National League
Stan Musial   St. Louis Cardinals

ROOKIE OF THE YEAR
ALVIN DARK BOSTON BRAVES

HOME RUN LEADERS
RALPH KINER PITTSBURGH PIRATES
JOHN MIZE NEW YORK YANKEES

BATTING CHAMPIONS
NATIONAL LEAGUE
STAN MUSIAL ST. LOUIS
AMERICAN LEAGUE
TED WILLIAMS BOSTON

- Legendary Negro League Pitcher, **Satchel Paige**, Makes His Major League Debut With The Cleveland Indians And Shuts Out The White Sox 5-0. He Finishes The Season With A 6-1 Record And 2.48 ERA.

- The 10-Team Negro American League Is The Only Segregated Association In Baseball After The Dissolution Of The Negro National League.

- **Leo Durocher** Resigns As Manager Of Brooklyn Dodgers And Accepts Job With New York Giants.

- Detroit Tiger Pitcher **Bob Lemon** Throws First No-Hitter Recorded In Detroit's 26 League Years And The First Night No-Hitter In American League History.

- **Harold "Pie" Traynor**, Pittsburgh Pirates Great Third Baseman And Hitter Of The 20's And 30's, Is Inducted Into The Baseball Hall Of Fame In Cooperstown, New York.

1948

New York Yankees at Spring Training

Joe Page among the pitchers warming those winning arms.

Bucky Harris predicts another championship season.

It's hard work and exercise for **Yogi Berra** as he gets ready for a catch.

George Stirnweiss (*right*) **and Phil Rizutto** (*left*) spell double play trouble.

Base stealing exercises are definitely part of the workout.

Joe DiMaggio gets his turn to slug one out.

WHAT A YEAR IT WAS!

It looks like old times with **"Lippy" Durocher** back as manager of the "Bums."

Brooklyn Bums Begin Spring Training

Veteran **Pee Wee Reese** is back at shortstop.

Jackie Robinson is still candidate for first base although there's talk of shifting him to second.

Much depends on young **Ralph Branca** who aided the Dodgers in their pennant drive last year.

Bragen, Hodges and **Edwards** discuss the coming season and pitches.

The team will miss **Eddie Stankey** who is recovering from pneumonia and being nursed back to health by his wife.

BASKETBALL

NCAA CHAMPIONSHIP
University Of Kentucky Beats
Baylor University 58-42

BASKETBALL ASSOCIATION OF AMERICA (BAA) CHAMPIONS
Baltimore Bullets (vs. Philadelphia Warriors)

BAA SCORING LEADER
Max Zaslofsky (Baltimore) 1,007 Points

NATIONAL BASKETBALL LEAGUE CHAMPIONS
The Minneapolis Lakers (vs. Rochester Royals)

- FOUR NBL TEAMS MERGE WITH BAA FORMING THE NBA.

- THE HARLEM GLOBETROTTERS BEAT NBL CHAMPS 61-59.

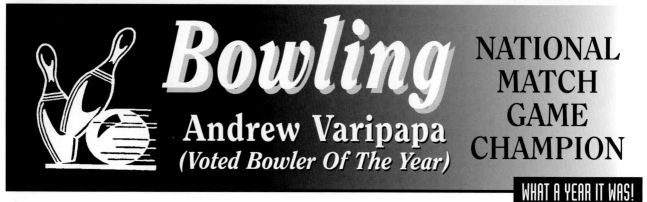

Bowling
Andrew Varipapa
(Voted Bowler Of The Year)

NATIONAL
MATCH
GAME
CHAMPION

WHAT A YEAR IT WAS!

1948

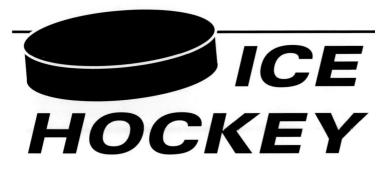
ICE HOCKEY

CALDER MEMORIAL
(Rookie Of The Year)
JIM McFADDEN

• • • • • • • • • • • • • • • • •

LADY BYNG MEMORIAL TROPHY
(Most Gentlemanly Player)
BUDDY O'CONNOR New York Rangers
(Also Most Valuable Player)

Toronto Maple Leafs Win National League Championship Beating Detroit Red Wings 4-0 And Take Stanley Cup

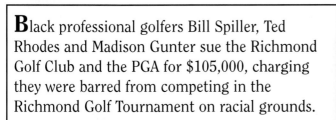
GOLF

Black professional golfers Bill Spiller, Ted Rhodes and Madison Gunter sue the Richmond Golf Club and the PGA for $105,000, charging they were barred from competing in the Richmond Golf Tournament on racial grounds.

The U.S. Golf Association bars "Babe" Didrikson Zaharias from the National Golf Open, ruling the tournament is restricted to men.

CHAMPIONS

MASTERS
Claude Harmon

U.S. AMATEUR
Willie Turnesa

U.S. OPEN-Men
Ben Hogan
(wins with a record 5 under par)

U.S. OPEN-Women
"Babe" Zaharias

PROFESSIONAL GOLFERS
Ben Hogan

BRITISH OPEN
Henry Cotton

Fans brave rains and show up for the exciting $169,000 Santa Anita Handicap—one of the richest stakes in the racing world.

Red Skelton is among the 62,000 spectators who show up for the running.

Mr. & Mrs. **Edgar Bergen** and **Gail Patrick** discuss horses as they line up for the race.

Betty Grable and **Harry James** are among other celebrities who gather for a day at the races.

Lou Costello says that picking the winner is a pipe.

Mr. and Mrs. **Don Ameche**.

WHAT A YEAR IT WAS!

Talon, wearing #1, is the number one favorite to win and with **Eddie Arcaro** riding, takes the lead in the homestretch and wins the race at Santa Anita.

HORSERACING

EDDIE ARCARO **Captures Triple Crown Riding "Citation" To Belmont Stakes, Preakness And Kentucky Derby Wins.**

JOHNNY LONGDEN **Wins Honors As Leading Rider As He Becomes First American Jockey To Ride More Than 3,000 Winners.**

HORSE OF THE YEAR: ***"CITATION"***

Rose Bowl

93,000 Fans Turn Out In Pasadena To Watch Michigan And Southern California Compete In Annual Rose Bowl Championship.

Elliott gets away for Michigan and racks up 18 yards before USC can pull him down.

Michigan won the first Rose Bowl contest 46 years ago and with Bob Chappuis passing, they are heavy favorites to win again.

It's Michigan's big day and they wind up winning 49-0.

WHAT A YEAR IT WAS!

FOOTBALL

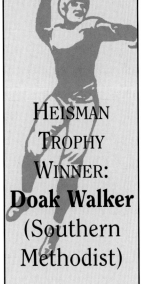

PHILADELPHIA EAGLES Beat CHICAGO CARDINALS 7-0 Winning National Football League Championship

NUMBER ONE NFL DRAFT CHOICE: **Harry Gilmer**, QB, Alabama (Team: Washington)

HEISMAN TROPHY WINNER: **Doak Walker** (Southern Methodist)

ARMY And NAVY Play To 21-21 Tie

Yale Appoints **Levi Jackson** To Coach Football Team Making Him First Negro To Be Chosen

Sailboats compete in the annual Lipton Cup Classic.

While the rest of the country faces winter's snow, ice and frozen pipes, these sailors take full advantage of Florida's beautiful weather.

At the Bellevue-Stratford
in Philadelphia

• In the Stratford Garden of Philadelphia's historic Bellevue-Stratford Hotel, as in so many of the distinctive places throughout the country, Webster Cigars are making a little history, too . . . for, today, more Websters are smoked than any other high-grade cigar (cigars selling from 15c up)! This success story is based on the unvarying blend that gives Websters such a dependable, satisfying flavor.

• There are five different sizes of Websters, selling from 15c to 35c. But, regardless of price or size, *every* Webster is made of 100% long Havana, bound in top-quality Broadleaf and wrapped in finest Connecticut Shade-grown. Sold wherever fine cigars are sold.

WEBSTER CIGARS
EXECUTIVE AMERICA'S TOP CIGAR

ADV. BY N. W. AYER

Golden Wedding, 15c   •   Chico, 15c   •   Queens, 18c   •   Fancy Tales, 25c   •   Directors, 35c

A PRODUCT OF THE WEBSTER TOBACCO COMPANY, INC., NEW YORK

BOXING

Champion JOE LOUIS Scores An 11th-Round Knockout Against JERSEY JOE WALCOTT Retaining His Title.

✺

JOE LOUIS Retires After Fighting 25 Title Bouts Since 1937.

✺ 20-Year Old SAM BAROUDI Dies In Chicago Hospital Of A Brain Hemorrhage After Boxing Match With Light-Heavyweight Contender EZZARD CHARLES. National Boxing Association Rules That Following A Knockdown A Boxer Must Take An Eight-Second Count Before Resuming Match.

✺ GUS LESNEVICH Retains World Light-Heavyweight Title Knocking Out BILLY FOX In The First Round.

✺ French Boxer MARCEL CERDAN Becomes The First Non-American Middleweight Champion Of The Century When Current Title Holder TONY ZALE Fails To Respond To 12th-Round Bell.

✺ World Featherweight Champion WILLIE PEP Knocks Out HUMBERTO SIERRA Retaining The Championship.

CAR RACING

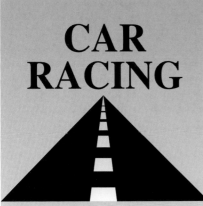

MAURI ROSE of South Bend, Indiana becomes third man in racing history to win the Indy 500 three times driving his *Blue Crown Special* and establishes record-breaking average time of 119.813 m.p.h.

GOING TO THE DOGS

At Doggydom's most prestigious event, the Westminster Dog Show, **CHAMPION ROCK RIDGE NIGHT ROCKET**, a Bedlington Terrier, wins Top Dog Award. The first of his breed to ever win best in show, the "Champ" is also the second dog in history to win both the indoor Westminster and the outdoor Morris & Essex show.

MOTORCYCLING

Riding a British "Vincent" which saw speeds of 140 m.p.h., 47-year old **ROLAND FREE** breaks world's motorcycle speed record clocking in at 150.855 m.p.h. in Salt Flats, Utah.

U.S. FINISHES THIRD WITH ITS STRONGEST SHOWING EVER IN THE WINTER OLYMPICS

Gretchen Fraser of the American Team pushes off in the Women's Slalom.

Her form is perfect as she twists and turns between the flags.

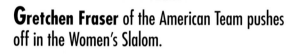

Gretchen zips across the finish line in winning time and brings joy to her teammates.

Gretchen scores 15 points for the U.S., the most points scored by any American in the games.

ICE SKATING

WORLD FIGURE SKATING CHAMPIONSHIP

Men:	Dick Button (U.S.)
Women:	Barbara Ann Scott (Canada)

U.S. NATIONAL

Men:	Dick Button (U.S.)
Women:	Gretchen Merrill

CANADIAN NATIONAL

Men:	Wallace E. Diestelmeyer
Women:	Barbara Ann Scott

Canada's **Barbara Ann Scott** exceeds the expectations of a host of admirers as they see her flash new brilliance in winning the Women's Figure Skating title.

Beauty and talent prove unbeatable as Barbara Ann displays the skill which made her undisputed queen of the flashing blades.

Miss Scott and her teammates bask in this moment of great glory.

Fans enthusiastically applaud as 18-year old American skater **Richard Button** of Englewood, New Jersey hits the ice.

First in Men's Figure Skating and already European title holder, Button surprises even his most ardent fans by making a clean sweep of both Figure and Free skating giving one of the most amazing exhibitions ever for the American Team.

Along with Miss Fraser's skiing victories and firsts in other events, Button's triumph puts the United States in third place, only a few points behind the winning Swedish team. Competing against the world's most talented athletes, it's the strongest showing any American team has made in the Winter Olympics.

"A SNACK AFTER THE MOVIES," by Stevan Dohanos. Number 14 in the series "Home Life in America," by noted American illustrators.

Beer belongs...enjoy it

In this home-loving land of ours . . . in this America of kindliness, of friendship, of good-humored tolerance . . . perhaps no beverages are more "at home" on more occasions than good American beer and ale.

For beer is the kind of beverage Americans like. It belongs—to pleasant living, to good fellowship, to sensible moderation. And our right to enjoy it, this too belongs—to our own American heritage of personal freedom.

AMERICA'S BEVERAGE OF MODERATION

SUMMER OLYMPICS

- 6,000 athletes from 59 nations compete in the XIV Olympiad in London.

- United States wins 38 gold medals, sweeping swimming events and emerging number one overall gold medal winner with Sweden and France following with 16 and 10 respectively.

- Record time in 10,000 Meter run: **Emil Zatopek**

- 30-year old Dutch housewife **Fanny Blankers-Koen** wins a record-breaking four gold medals in 100-Meter and 200-Meter Sprints, 80-Meter Hurdles and 400-Meter Relay.

- 17-year old Californian **Bob Mathias** wins the Decathlon and breaks the record by becoming the youngest man in history to win a Track and Field gold medal.

- James E. Sullivan Trophy Winner: **Robert Mathias** (track)

WINTER OLYMPICS

- St. Moritz hosts the Fifth Winter Olympics—the first since 1936.

- Val d'Isere's 21-year old **Henri Oreiller** is the only athlete to earn two gold medals in the Winter Olympics, winning Men's Downhill and Alpine Combined Event.

- The U.S. wins its first gold medal in Figure Skating, but finishes third in the Olympics behind Sweden and Switzerland.

WINTER OLYMPIC WINNERS

FIGURE SKATING

Men's Singles	Women's Singles
Dick Button (U.S.)	**Barbara Ann Scott** (Canada)

DOWNHILL SKIING

Men's	Women's
Henri Oreiller (France)	**Hedi Schlunegger** (Switzerland)

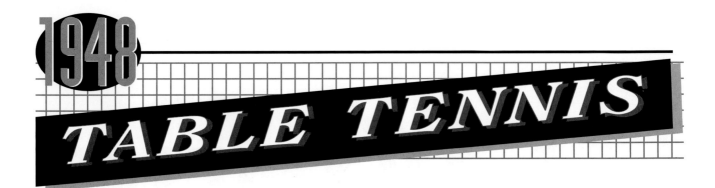

TABLE TENNIS

- ○ **WORLD TABLE TENNIS CHAMPIONSHIPS**—Wembly Stadium, London. 10,000 Spectators Attend.

- ○ Czechoslovakian Men's Team Retains Swaythling Cup Beating 24 Countries.

- ○ England's Women's Team Keeps The Corbillion Cup, Winning Over 15 Countries.

- ○ Plastic Balls Are Tested To Replace Celluloid.

THE CHAMPIONS

Men's Singles: Richard Bergmann (England) over Bohumil Vana (Czechoslovakia)

Women's Singles: Gizi Farkas (Hungary)

Men's Doubles: Bohumil Vana & Ladislav Stipek (Czechoslovakia)

Women's Doubles: Vera Dace Thomas & Peggy Franks (England)

World Billiard Championships

THREE CUSHION CROWN	Willie Hoppe (vs. Ezequiel Navarra)
POCKET TITLE	Willie Mosconi (vs. Andrew Ponzi)

PASSINGS

Former world light-heavyweight champion boxer **Jack Delaney**, whose winnings include 35 knockouts, dies at age 48.

Herbert Pennock, who, in twenty-two years as a major league pitcher helped win the World Series five times, dies in Manhattan at age 53.

27-year old **Stanley Mauldin**, tackle for the NFL's Chicago Cardinals, dies from a heart attack after a football game.

FAMOUS BIRTHS

Terry Bradshaw

Peggy Fleming

Steve Garvey

Bryant Gumbel

CHAMPIONS — TENNIS — 1948

U.S. NATIONAL SINGLES
Men: Poncho Gonzales (over Eric Sturgess)
Women: Margaret du Pont (over Louise Brough)

U.S. DOUBLES
Men: Gardnar Mulloy & William F. Talbert
Women: Louise Brough & Margaret du Pont

WIMBLEDON
Men: Robert Faulkenburg (over John Bromwich)
Women: Louise Brough (over Doris Hart)

FOREST HILLS
Jack Kramer Beats Bobby Riggs Taking 21st Pro Tennis Title.

U.S. Team, Gardnar Mulloy And William F. Talbert, Beats Australian Team, Colin Long & Billy Sidwel, 5-0 Winning Davis Cup.

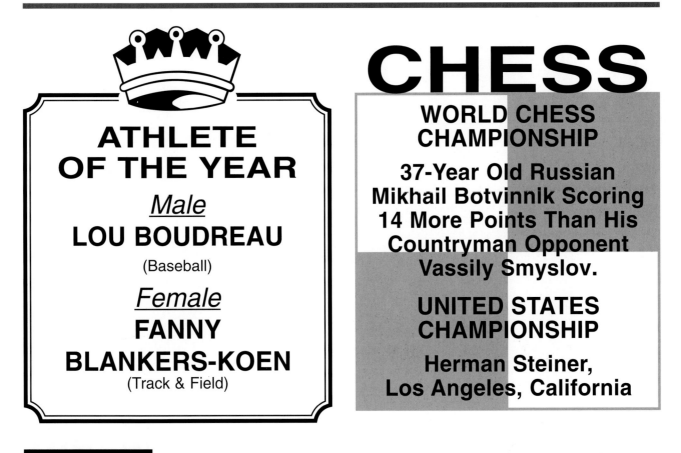

ATHLETE OF THE YEAR

Male
LOU BOUDREAU
(Baseball)

Female
FANNY BLANKERS-KOEN
(Track & Field)

CHESS

WORLD CHESS CHAMPIONSHIP

37-Year Old Russian Mikhail Botvinnik Scoring 14 More Points Than His Countryman Opponent Vassily Smyslov.

UNITED STATES CHAMPIONSHIP

Herman Steiner, Los Angeles, California

1948 WAS A GREAT YEAR, BUT...

THE BEST IS YET TO COME!